Cyberspace and Security

A Fundamentally New Approach

REVISED EDITION

VICTOR SHEYMOV

Cyberbooks Publishing

ISBN-10: 0985893001
ISBN-13: 9780985893002
Library of Congress Control Number: 2012944412
CreateSpace Independent Publishing Platform
North Charleston, South Carolina

Second, Revised, Edition, September 2013
(now including a new Part IV)

First Printing, July 2012

The author welcomes feedback, questions, and media requests
contact@cyberbookspublishing.com
www.cyberbookspublishing.com

To all inventors who break the barriers of conventional thinking, despite the tremendous power of entrenched bureaucracies.

Acknowledgments

I would like to acknowledge my dear friend the late Jim Dyer, a Distinguished Member of the Cryptos Society, and a legend at the NSA. Jim was the first person with whom I discussed my invention of the VCC method of communications, the first to appreciate it and to encourage me to further the concept.

I was fortunate to have the talent and experience of my editor and agent, Roger Jellinek, contributing to this book.

I would like to express my gratitude to Sergey Zelensky for his valuable scientific editorial advice.

I am grateful to Olga Sheymov who applied her talent to designing this book's cover.

I also would like to express my gratitude to my patent lawyer Carlos Villamar for his exceptionally competent work with my patents in cybersecurity.

Contents

PART III. CYBERSECURITY

**PART IV
COHERENT DEFENSE OF LARGE
SOVEREIGN CYBER SYSTEMS**

Preface

Breaches of cyber security are a topic of increasingly popular concern. We refer to them almost as to natural disasters. We acknowledge the inevitability of catastrophic failure. Experts routinely report on the escalating danger, and demand "preparedness."

We have now been staring at the cyber security problem for a quarter of a century without any effective action. At best, our response is like waving a small shield and a big sword against a major storm. With the small shield, we are trying to protect ourselves from the wind, rain, and hail; with the big sword, we are hoping to scare the storm away.

This has not worked; and it will not work.

This book addresses cyber security by analyzing the real and different nature of cyberspace. It clarifies how the security methods we designed for the physical world are futile in cyberspace.

The book's comprehensive multidisciplinary approach suggests a fundamentally new approach to security in cyberspace and lays out a foundation for effective and reliable solutions to the problem.

Victor Sheymov
Washington DC, July 2012

Introduction

Running Out Of Time

As a country, we are slowly coming to the realization that we are vulnerable. Hopefully, not too slowly. We are almost subconsciously accustomed to knowing that we are vulnerable to a nuclear attack by a very powerful potential adversary; luckily, there are only two of them on this planet. We are getting used to the realization that we are vulnerable to a possible collapse of the globalized monetary system. But we have yet to realize that we are vulnerable to a cyber attack that could be more damaging than anything except a massive nuclear strike. The most startling fact is that such an attack could be delivered by an individual or a small group with a few thousand dollars and access to nothing more than the Internet. This aspect is politely called "asymmetric warfare," but in fact it represents the failure of our security technology.

The estimated annual cost of global cyber crimes is $960 billion, but that is just a small part of the threat. Damage to critical infrastructure and major industrial assets can easily surpass that, not to mention the potential of massive loss of life. We are beginning to realize that a cyber attack can literally incapacitate our critical infrastructure. Cyber attacks can explode oil refineries and chemical factories, clog up our streets and make emergency services powerless if they themselves are still available, and leave our houses without heating and air conditioning—or even blown up by the manipulation of gas distribution systems. If this list is not impressive enough, it can be very easily extended. And the reality is that at this time we are not doing much to defend against such attacks.

Let us make a quick review of some typical and specific cyber dangers we are facing.

Financial Sector and Finances of Corporations

The checks and balances method of bookkeeping, invented centuries ago, was simple and effective. A business owner employed different people for accounts payable and accounts receivable and made sure they did not collude. At the end of the day, the owner calculated the difference between the two accounts and compared the result with the cash on hand for the day. If there was a discrepancy, somebody had made a mistake or somebody had stolen money, and the owner knew exactly how much. This was a fundamental concept, and other more modern methods are variations of the same theme. The basic concept of this method is to separate some financial processes and to *independently* check the balance.

The difference now is that there are a huge number of rapid transactions going on. Computers can handle that traffic, but what computers cannot handle is the lack of *independence* in the processes. This is precisely what any hacker worth his salt can exploit. Hackers can modify the data in both payables and receivables so the balance stays correct and alarms are not triggered, while money can be diverted somewhere at the hacker's direction. Theft has occurred; detection has failed. It appears that many financial managers do not understand this vulnerability, while there are clear signs that criminals are taking advantage of this situation. At least in one recent criminal case, the alleged perpetrators included a hacker and an accountant intimately familiar with a particular company's accounting system and procedures.

Industrial Control Systems

Practically all industrial enterprises use computers to control their processes. Most enterprises possess large amounts of energy necessary for performing their technological functions on their premises, such as oil, gas, chemicals, electricity, etc. The most energy-intensive facilities are oil refineries, fuel tank farms, gas processing and distribution enterprises, all types of power stations, and chemical factories. Attacking these facilities would be a dream come true for terrorists, our sworn enemies. Accidents at these facilities are visually spectacular, often come with human casualties, attract guaranteed media attention and great public concern, and trigger political tension.

Over many years of technological development, engineers have understood such industrial perils and developed safety systems that make such events highly unlikely. Computers made these safety measures more effective. Practically all these industrial safety systems are based on the same principle: *independent* verification of process parameters performed by a system. For example, the pressure of a chemical reaction in a vessel is automatically maintained by one system, but *independently* verified by another, and safety measures are performed when the parameter is out of a safe range. This concept works very well—until a cyber attack comes into play. An attacker can take control of both computers, cause an accident, and preclude the safety system from noticing it, thus eliminating the *independence* factor. The recent attack of the Stuxnet computer worm on Iranian nuclear fuel processing centrifuges, and a demo destruction of a power generator by hacking at the Idaho National Lab, are classic examples.

Power Grid

All of our power distribution is computerized. The power distribution control systems, along with the industrial control systems cited above, are often called SCADA (Supervisory Control And Data Acquisition) systems. They share the same functional principle: parameters maintained by one system are verified by another, making *independent* measurements. A power grid can be similarly attacked, and power distribution can be disrupted.

So a cyber attack can cause any possible malfunction in a system when all safety measures have failed. The significant and often overlooked point regarding damage to the SCADA systems is that a cyber attack can do more damage than a freak accident, even with all the safety measures failed. The difference is that, in addition to causing an accident, a cyber attack can also substantially damage the computers, making recovery lengthy indeed, especially in a case like a power grid attack.

Another important and often overlooked aspect is that many computers are infected by malware well before this malware is triggered. It means that many of our critical infrastructure computers already contain "cyber bombs" that are waiting to be triggered at the time chosen by the attacker to maximize the damage. This malware is extremely difficult to detect, and on a large scale such detection is a practical impossibility. Furthermore, disconnecting computers from the Internet in most cases would be ineffective, since malware can easily reconnect the computer to the Internet if a proper hardware and a wireless access are present, and they usually are. So we are sitting on multiple bombs embedded in our critical infrastructure at the mercy of multiple unknown attackers.

Thus we are facing a grim reality that we do not fully comprehend, and not much has been done about it so far. Our vulnerability has not improved over the years; indeed, it has deteriorated. The technology of cyber attacks has advanced more than technology of computer security. Let us review how we got into this situation and, more importantly, how to get out of it.

We cannot blame designers of the Internet for security problems—security was not on their task list. Quite to the contrary, the main goals were to provide survivability of the networks in a case of a partial area loss from an event like a nuclear strike, and to establish free exchange of information over the network.

The popularity of the Internet quickly led to cyber attacks. We realized the danger and developed our defenses, largely based on variations of a firewall. It does not work, and never did; in fact, it has been mathematically proven that any firewall can be penetrated; furthermore, any firewall can be penetrated in an unlimited number of ways. In the high-tech world, if something does not work within three to four years in the mainstream, it's dead. Remarkably, we have been clinging to the firewall regardless for a quarter of a century. Why? We did not come up with an alternative.

Instead, we engaged in a series of four nontechnical solutions:

- **Defense by marketing**
- **Defense by politics**
- **Defense by deterrence**
- **Defense by semantics**

Defense by marketing. Marketers of numerous firewall manufacturers did wonderful job. "Firewall" sounds solid and reassuring. Actually, "fig leaf" protection is a far more accurate description of the firewall technology. No matter, we kept manufacturing, selling, and buying firewalls, happily using the electronic version of the proverbial king's clothing.

Defense by politics. As technical measures did not work, we started the second phase. We tried to contemplate legal obstacles to cyber attacks, both domestically and abroad, by pressuring other countries to "crack down" on cyber criminals. This approach was quickly proved largely ineffective and quietly stopped. The latest attempt to revive this approach was made at a London conference for cyber security at the end of October 2011, and it was promptly rejected by most participants, notably the British.

Defense by deterrence. Some politicians and generals fighting the traditional "last war" tried to resurrect the Cold War approach of strategic deterrence. This was a spectacularly misguided effort. During the Cold War, we knew exactly who the offender would be, and the threat of swift retaliation would follow. In cyberspace, we can sometimes, but not always, discover who the offender is. However, we can never be certain. In fact, often we don't even know there even is an offender because we often cannot detect an attack that has already succeeded.

Furthermore, there is a wide range of a potential deterrence measures. At one end of the spectrum, a mother's notion of not giving a new bike for a guy's fifteenth birthday is deterrent enough. At the other end, for an al Qaeda terrorist, a potential death penalty would not be deterrence but a badge of honor. Who are we supposed to deter and how? Luckily, the idea of defense by deterrence was sent back to happy retirement.

Defense by semantics. Under pressure of the facts, in the last few years it has become possible to say, off the record, that the firewall methodology does not work. This was progress—at least it was a triumph for free speech. So the second nontechnical solution tried, incidentally usually performed by technical "experts," was defense by semantics. A large number of new terms and acronyms flooded the market, and we came to a point where computer security lingo became an alien foreign language that everybody speaks but nobody understands. However, the facts were still pressing, and the danger has become too obvious to ignore.

We finally have begun to realize that we have run out of nontechnological solutions to the technological problem. This book establishes that our legacy computer security systems are not effective for a simple reason: we tried to protect cyberspace objects using security methods developed for physical space. These two spaces are so different that methods effective in one do not necessarily work in the other. Our physical space security methods are generally static. We tried to export them into cyberspace, and experience tells us they are not effective there. In order to adapt to the highly dynamic environment of cyberspace, we need to base our security on dynamics and secure virtualization.

The mainstream government experts are finally beginning to realize and acknowledge that fundamentally different principles of cyber security must be developed, and they are now requesting the development of "dynamic" systems. For instance, the Department of Homeland Security recently stated: "It is now clear that static systems present a substantial advantage to attackers." The US Army's CERDEC (Communications-Electronics Research, Development) stated: "The CERDEC is interested in proposals for MORPHINATOR to develop cyber maneuver technologies including Port hopping and IP hopping...."

The fact that government experts are beginning to request development of new dynamic technologies is encouraging. But we need to understand that we are living free of a major cyber attack on borrowed time. We are extremely vulnerable, and we do not know how wide is the window of time we have to protect ourselves. Given all the issues raised above, this book explains the difference between true cyber security and the failed legacy approaches to computer security. The reader will discover that cyberspace is so different from our physical space that security there has to be approached from a fundamentally different direction.

This book consists of four parts: I, Security; II, Cyberspace; III, Cyber security; and IV, Coherent Defense of Large Cyber Systems. In this book we will

- Review the history of what we have been doing to establish access security.

- Analyze the nature of cyberspace and its fundamental difference from our physical world.

- Analyze the applicability of our legacy security measures to cyberspace.

- Determine what has been fundamentally wrong with our legacy approach to cyber security.

- Present a new approach to security that is effective in cyberspace.

Given all the considerations above, a natural question arises: We have enough trouble protecting a few computers, so how can we possibly protect millions of them, connected in very large systems? Part IV, new to this Second Edition, deals directly with this issue. It analyses different types of large systems, describes the difficulties of protecting them, and suggests solutions.

Part IV also shows that massive monitoring of cyberspace, while being extremely expensive, can bring only very short-term benefits, if any at all. In the longer term it is not technically feasible to achieve security by that method

PART I
Security

Chapter 1

SECURITY

1.1 Definitions

A standard first dictionary definition of "security" is "freedom from danger." "Danger" or "threat," as it is often labeled, has to be present or assumed to be present—otherwise there is no need for security. In recent years, "threat" has conventionally been defined by security professionals as the sum of the opposition's capability, intent (will), and opportunity, and can be expressed thus:

- **Threat = Capability + Intent (will) + Opportunity**

Indeed, without a capability, an attack cannot take place. An attacker must possess a specific capability for a specific attack. For instance, the Afghan Taliban cannot carry out a nuclear missile attack on the United States even if they have full intent and an opportunity. Intent or will is also a necessary ingredient. North Korea has the capability for a nuclear strike on South Korea, but many factors keep their will in check. Similarly, Iran may have a capability to attack a defenseless American recreational sailboat in its territorial waters, and be perfectly willing to do so, but American recreational sailors just do not go there, providing no opportunity.

It should be noted that the definition above is quite specific and should be applied to every specific adversary or potential adversary and then integrated for the multitude of one's adversaries. Furthermore, applying this formula usually does not produce precise results since ingredients such as "capability" and "opportunity" are usually not known exactly and often are just assumed. A classic example of this is the infamous case of Iraq's weapons of mass destruction as justification of the last Iraq war.

The first recorded breach of security occurred in the Garden of Eden. Apparently, there was a sense of threat, and Cherubim guarding it with flaming swords were the security measures taken. However, the security measures were insufficient, and that allowed the serpent to infiltrate the Garden of Eden and do his ungodly deed.

In fact, there is no perfect security. We can only provide degrees of protection (i.e., if there is a threat, risk is always present, though its level may vary. Often this is reflected in the statement that risk is a combination of threat and vulnerability:

- **Risk = Threat + Vulnerability**

This looks logical since vulnerability means exposure to a certain threat. This also leads to the assertion that:

- **Vulnerability is a deficiency of protection against a specific attack**.

A reasonably comprehensive definition of security would probably be something like:

- **A set of measures that eliminate, or at least alleviate the probability of destruction, theft, or damage to a being, an object, a process, or data, including the revelation of a process, or of the content of information.**

The important point here is that a security measure is a response to a threat, rather than an attack. This simply means that security measures must be established before an attack takes place; in other words, it should be proactive. If there is an attack, it is too late to establish security; that is the time for security measures that have already been established to actually counter the attack.

There is a fair amount of misunderstanding regarding security. Many people put security cameras in their homes and genuinely think these cameras are security measures. Actually, a security camera in a home environment can only be a forensic tool, not a security tool (unless you have 24/7 monitoring personnel and a SWAT team on standby within a few minutes' ride). The camera would not save you from a determined intruder in any way, but it could be a great tool for the police to find the party who burglarized your home and/or killed you.

- **A security measure is a reaction to a threat, rather than an attack.**

Real security measures should be established in reaction to the threat, not in reaction to an attack. Police searching for a burglary suspect is not a security measure any more than forensic work can prevent the hacking of a computer system (at least in the first approximation; it could be argued that catching the suspect would prevent future crimes).

- **Real security measures have to be proactive, not reactive.**

"Safety" and "security" are often used interchangeably. For the sake of clarity, we will assume here that "safety" refers to addressing threats of natural or unintended man-made threats. An earthquake or an accidental building fire are good examples. Then we will use "security" to address intentional man-made threats. We'll exclude security regarding threats of open military confrontations, since they represent a military subject that is well studied. (However, we note that military security does also deal with subversive threats to military forces.) Thus for our purposes here:

- "Security" is a response to an intentional subversive or clandestine man-made threat.

1.2 Legacy Security Systems

Given the physical nature of our space, interactions in it tend to be physical. Much damage in this space occurs as a result of physical interactions, governed by the known laws of physics. Our instinct is to provide security by establishing a physical obstacle, such as a wall high enough to prevent unauthorized access. The derivatives of that assumption are fortresses, bunkers, etc. For centuries, we have been taught to fortify whatever is to be protected, so we are conditioned to think in terms of fortification for security.

There are two other kinds of physical security systems that have been tried: security by hiding and security by movement. Security by hiding has a fairly limited application, mainly due to two characteristic situations: physical space is limited (and available hiding places with specific requirements are also limited); and secondly, a well-hidden object is usually not readily available, and keeping its hiding place and its particulars secret while accessing the object is often difficult. For example, country X's military may try to hide the location of its unit armed with missiles. However, the need to supply and communicate with this unit and its personnel usually soon reveal its location.

Security by movement also has limited application, mainly in a military environment. The main reason is that movement in physical space is difficult and expensive. It requires a lot of energy to overcome forces of gravity and friction, and it also requires sophisticated control-communications capabilities that are not easy in themselves. For instance, in a presatellite era, a ship at sea could be difficult to find and attack, but its communications limitations presented difficulties for control, while every communication provided the potential to reveal its position to a potential attacker. In other words, the ship's location could be discovered as soon as it started communicating.

The definition of security above gives a very generalized feel for security as a subject of study. However, there is no such thing as a general threat, thus it is not possible to establish general security.

Security should be addressed by devising concrete, specific measures to address specific threats. For instance, fortifying a facility would not help much against suspected or confirmed intercepts of telephone communications on international lines.

This brings the identification of threats to the forefront, as we consider how to devise our security measures. Threat usually comes from a source, i.e., an adversary. Let us review the threat formula from before:

- **Threat = Capability + Intent (will) + Opportunity**

Indeed, an adversary can have a capability to inflict damage on what we are protecting, but may be reluctant to so. A classic example of that is the MAD (Mutually Assured Destruction) policy during the Cold War. Both sides had the capability to execute a nuclear strike, but neither dared to do so, fearing the certain consequences. On the other hand, *al -Qaeda* may be very determined and eager to conduct a major cyber attack on critical US infrastructure, but it does not have the capability do so, at least not yet. This highlights the necessity of careful study of the adversary or a potential adversary in terms of both capabilities and will. This is an intelligence function, and it cannot be emphasized strongly enough that if we want to have any success in security we must have successful, relevant intelligence. Probably the most famous military example in recent history is the D-Day invasion. If the Germans had had better intelligence, the invasion would have been doomed, with unpredictable consequences on a global scale.

One of the main goals of intelligence is to identify a threat before it becomes an attack. If the Trojans had considered the construction of the Trojan horse (which they should have done) and assumed that it might be loaded with armed men, the Trojan War would surely have ended very differently. It should be noted that intelligence here is meant to include the intelligence of the "user," or "customer," in other words a decision-maker. Indeed, it can be noted that the **level of intelligence cannot exceed the intelligence level of the user**. For example, Soviet intelligence discovered that Germany would attack the Soviet Union on June 22, 1941. This was extremely valuable intelligence, but it was ignored by Stalin on "high-level political" grounds, and any preparations were forbidden in order not to "provoke" the Germans. The result was that the Soviet army was in a disorderly retreat, and by the New Year, German armies were directly threatening Moscow.

These considerations define the two principal roles of intelligence:

Defense—with the mission to discover, detect, and identify potential threats before they are developed, so the defenders can establish countermeasures to prevent and sabotage an attack;

Offense—with the mission to identify the existing vulnerabilities of a target and develop new vulnerabilities, preferably those that can be utilized by the customer's existing offensive capabilities.

With these general considerations regarding security in mind, it is useful to take a look at different aspects of security related to different types of threat. Generally speaking, threats are developed by attacking parties, and the defending parties are in a response mode. Successful intelligence not only enables the defender to shorten the gap between the development of an attack venue and the development of an effective countermeasure. This also makes it clear that defensive work is usually more challenging than offensive work, since the attacker has the advantage of a choice of venue, place, and time of the attack and can concentrate its power in one attack, while the defender has to be ready to counter numerous possibilities.

Most security efforts designed to protect material assets, such as valuables and money, are directed at preventing an unauthorized removal of the assets. The more restricted the authorized access, the easier the security task becomes. Fort Knox is a classic example of this fortress approach to security.

A totally different set of priorities evolved regarding information security. Since well before the cyberspace age, information security was always a special case. Although prevention of an attack is a priority, a significant effort has been devoted to measures detecting unauthorized access to information. This mission has always made information security very different from asset security. Furthermore, it is difficult to make a copy of a hard asset such as a gold bar. If one wants to steal it, one has to steal the original. With information, a copy usually is sufficient (unless someone needs an original for, say, legal reasons). Copying is easy with a small amount of information. Memorizing a short letter, for example is not too difficult, assuming the attacker can read the language. There were methods of copying that allowed the attacker to deal with larger amounts of information. It became critically important to detect the fact that informational assets had been "leaked," even if information remained safely in place. This became the highest priority in military and intelligence operations, as well as in diplomacy. If a defender knew that his battle plan had become known to the enemy, he would design another plan (time permitting, of course). If, however, he was unaware of the "leak," a full-blown disaster would likely ensue. The development of computer technology has made intercepting and copying information increasingly easy, putting significant pressure on the defenders.

Thus one needs to distinguish between the security of an object and the security of data or of a process. Securing a vault full of gold is a very different task from securing a communication from a head of state to the country's ambassador in a remote country. While the two aspects often intersect, for our purposes we will concentrate mainly on data and communications security.

1.3 Communications and Computer Security in Physical Space

Information security existed well before the development of cyberspace and before the development of computers, but its methods were limited to physical space. Bearing in mind the main subject of this book, we will briefly review physical security of information here. We find four major aspects:

Information-related physical security. Physical security covers the most traditional types, like security of buildings, objects, and people. All these can be carriers or depositors of information. One of the important components of this category is physical access security. This aspect was in a relatively stable state for centuries, but the latest development in technology significantly changed the playing field. While this is not a cyber issue, we may see in the following chapters that access security can have a significant impact on cyber security. This is a still developing field, and while being outside of the scope of this book, it clearly deserves a depiction of its own.

Personnel security. The long-held maxim that the weakest point of any security system is a human element can probably be challenged by cyber security, but the fact remains that personnel security is also highly pertinent to cyber security.

Procedural security. Procedural security is a complex subject. It involves all aspects of security and requires rules and procedures to be followed in order to minimize overall security gaps, especially at the boundaries of different security aspects.

Technical security. It is important to realize this can have significant impact on cyber security, which we will address later, and on information/data security. Pertinent to computer and communications security, it has several elements that may be important for our purpose:

- **Electromagnetic (EM) field intercept/interference of computations and communications.** Most computers and communications devices are powered by electricity and work by manipulating electric currents. This process invariably produces an electromagnetic field. This field can be measured at significant distances from the source computer. This, in turn, creates an opening for an attacker to receive these EM fields and to decode the underlying process within the computer. Furthermore, this aspect can be taken to the next level: having analyzed these EM emanations, an attacker can emanate corresponding EM signals of his own, interfering with the work of the computer, since the computer receives these EM signals and may not be able to distinguish them from its own legitimate signals.

- **Acoustic intercept of conversations, as well as such processes as typing and printing.** This is a traditional field of "eavesdropping" that can be used against either conversations or acoustic components of some processes.
- **Vibrational intercept of conversations and communications.** This is a less traditional method but can be quite effective. For instance, some years ago someone came up with the cute idea of making "secure conversations rooms," basically large cubes with thick, clear plastic walls, floor, and ceiling that stood on large cubes of clear plastic within a larger room. The bright idea behind it was that any eavesdropping device or its wires would be visible through the clear plastic. The KGB had a field day with these "secure" plastic rooms, and their experts had a wholehearted laugh. Sure enough, these cubes protected the conversation held inside from the security-cleared people outside in the larger room. But the voice acoustic waves induced micro vibrations in the plastic walls of the "secure" rooms. These vibrations then traveled significant distances to well beyond the secure zone and were available to anybody with a decent accelerometer and the knowledge of how to make a high-quality recording of the conversation. This aspect of security in sensitive areas is sometimes missed, but it has to be addressed with appropriate care.

These fields are not only very different technically and technologically, but they often produce different or even contradictory requirements for security implementation at a particular facility. For instance, within a common Sensitive Compartmented Information Facility (SCIF), from an electromagnetic standpoint, security may require a particular piece of equipment to be placed close to a computer inside. At the same time, acoustic security considerations would require the same piece of machinery to be placed as far as possible from that computer. Furthermore, specific security requirements for these two considerations may make it difficult to satisfy both without a major redesign of the facility.

This example illustrates the fact that security considerations must be coordinated among different relevant security fields. The integration of a system with different security requirements for each of technical, physical, personnel, and procedural security can become a real challenge. On the one hand, multiple security measures have to address different specific multiple threats; on the other hand, all security measures have to be coordinated and integrated.

This dilemma becomes even more complex in places where critically important devices in physical space interact with cyberspace, as in cyber-physical systems. This will be addressed in later chapters.

Computer and communications security was addressed well before we built cyberspace and could be considered a mature field. Essentially, it is based on traditional methods of physical space security, i.e., fortification. We fortify buildings containing computers requiring security; we fortify points of access to computers; we implement access security; and we establish some personnel security policies. In addition to fortification, we sometimes encrypt data, which is a separate subject of discussion. All in all, we use well-known and tested methods of security that are based on laws of our physical space.

CHAPTER 2

ACCESS SECURITY—GENERAL

We will now take a look at physical access control security systems from a cryptographic perspective. This can be done more easily if we first review the cryptographic aspects of a mechanical device, such as a common pin tumbler door lock. While being much simpler to understand, it is based on the same principles as most of the current access security systems.

2.1 Basics of Crypto Systems

First, let us very briefly review the basics of a crypto system. A typical cryptographic system usually consists of an encryption/decryption algorithm and a key. For assessing the robustness of a crypto system, it is assumed that the algorithm is known to the opposition (a potential attacker). The theoretical robustness of the system is dependent on two factors: the strength of the algorithm and the length of the key. The strongest cryptographic protection known is the one-time-pad system. In this system, the algorithm is extremely simple: first, the sender converts the message from text to numbers; second, he adds every digit of the converted message to the corresponding digit of the key. The result is the encrypted message. The receiver applies the opposite process: first, he subtracts every digit of his copy of the key from corresponding digits of the encrypted message; second, he converts the resulting numerical message in the clear text. In this algorithm, the length of the key is equal to the length of the message. Both the sender and the receiver must have the same key. The key can be used only once (hence the name). While being unquestionably the most robust, this system has inherent practical limitations: it is only as good as the quality of the key (how random is "random"?) and it also requires a secure key distribution system. The complexity of the key distribution system grows exponentially with the volume of the data to be enciphered, and its security and reliability are inversely proportional to both, the volume of the keys and the number of participants.

The "theoretical" robustness is just that, theoretical. In practice, numerous factors can weaken the actual robustness. For instance, one major question is how random is the "random" key? This is a fundamental question and a potential danger for all cipher systems. This issue is extremely complex, and its details are heavily guarded by the relevant government agencies of several countries. For the purposes of this book, it suffices to say that every random key is not really random, thus creating an opening for an attack.

Another issue is the strength of the algorithm. For centuries, mathematicians have created the strongest possible algorithms for encryption systems, only to see them solved by the following generation of mathematicians. There are also many instances of a "shortcut" for an algorithm being discovered, creating a venue for an attack that has made it easier to recover either the contents of the encrypted data or the key (with essentially the same result).

A further aspect of the practical robustness of a crypto system is its implementation. Thus mathematicians analyze the mathematical concept of the system, but a real system in physical space is made of various physical components that do not necessarily exactly represent the mathematical algorithm, essentially corrupting the otherwise well-designed crypto system. This discrepancy permits a possible attack based on the actual physical elements of the system. This is why, in an evaluation of a crypto system by a competent authority, we often see the caveat "if properly implemented." This is not an empty bureaucratic phrase, but a warning of a real danger. This danger is amplified by the fact that the flaws found in encryption systems are often not published, leaving some party in a position of advantage and the defending party with a dangerous delusion of security. A classic example of this was when, during WWII, British GCHQ solved the German coding machine algorithm and the Allies knew the German submarine operations as well as the German High Command.

2.2 Mechanical Access Systems

Reviewing the security of physical access control from a cryptographic perspective, let us consider the common mechanical pin tumbler door lock, of which there are probably many millions in the world. The lock construction and the general shape of the key (common for all keys of this kind of lock) represent a crypto algorithm. The width, thickness, the groove in the blade, and the mechanism of the lock represent its crypto algorithm parameters, which are readily available to anyone interested. The height of the blade at different points represents the "secret" key that corresponds with the cuts in the pins. A better lock of this type often contains 6 pins that usually can be cut in fewer than 11 different locations, typically 6. The total number of possible key combinations for such a lock with 6 pin stacks and 6 bitting depths in a stack (i.e., the possible locations of a cut) is $6^6 = 46,656$.

So, the security of the lock is based on the correct choice out of 46,656 combinations. For a practical attacker, this may represent the inconvenient task of making a lot of keys and trying them. However, for a computer this is a small number to try with "brute force" (the term "brute force" in this context is meant in a cryptographic sense, using computer power to solve the calculation problem, and does not include breaking the lock or knocking the door down).

Another way of attacking this crypto system is to try to find a shortcut that will weaken the algorithm, making the process for defeating this system easier. One way is commonly known as a "pick." This is based on the fact that the manufacturing tolerances of the lock are sufficiently great that instead of all the pins holding the lock and preventing the cylinder from turning, only one pin is actually holding the cylinder at any time. By sequentially looking for and finding the "holding" pin, and then carefully manipulating the pin height with an appropriate tool, an attacker can open the lock by selecting the proper pin position on all 6 pins with no more than 6 manipulations. This means that the already low theoretical entropy level of 46,656 possible values of the key is further reduced to just 6. This is precisely what is referred to by the proviso "properly implemented." The term "entropy" here is a measure of uncertainty or "chaos" in the cryptographic system, i.e., an indicator of how difficult it is to guess it.

Interestingly, the security of this kind of lock is also significantly reduced in a system that employs "master keys," i.e., keys that can open a number of locks in a system utilizing individually different keys, such as are often deployed in office buildings and hotels. A master key that opens any lock in a system can be manufactured easily and cheaply without any special tools or skills, providing the maker has access to just one individual key within the system and a lock. In other words, in order to enter any room in a hotel with such a system of mechanical door locks, all an attacker needs is to check into any room and obtain that particular room key.

We have reviewed this simple example of a mechanical door key from a cryptographic perspective because this system is representative of the majority of mechanical access control security systems.

Thus to analyze an access control system we have to look at the following aspects:

- **The strength of the algorithm**
- **The length of the key**
- **The quality of the key (i.e., how random is its "random" sequence)**
- **The implementation of the algorithm**

And further:

- Is a key sample available to the attacker?
- Are shortcuts available that can weaken the algorithm?
- Does the implementation itself (e.g., the manufacturing process) create shortcuts?

In our example of the mechanical pin tumbler door lock, these questions can be answered as follows:

The strength of the algorithm: the algorithm is very simple and does not afford much room for developing a mathematical shortcut.

The length of the key: it is quite short, where the cuts can be represented by five numbers between 1and 6. With that key length, the algorithm would afford a level of entropy corresponding to the ratio of 1:46,656. Is that good or bad? It depends on the particular facts of the situation. Theoretically, with a brute force approach, it would take less than 46,657 tries to find the solution of 6 digits. For a computer, this is a really small number. For a practical attacker, it may be a different story. The effort required for a "try" is a factor. In our example, manufacturing 46,656 keys would be technically not too difficult, but the cost involved probably would not justify the possible benefit of opening the lock.

The quality of the key: the quality of the key is not a major factor here considering other means for an attack. Suppose an attacker knows that the 6-digit key has two identical digits. It would ease the brute force approach, but it might not make it preferable vis-à-vis other available venues.

The implementation of the algorithm: the key may be available to the attacker. If so, making a copy of the key is not too difficult, and the lock could be opened. This means the security of the lock is dependent at all times on physical security of the key. Shortcuts may be available, particularly when a lock belongs to a system with a master key. In this case, the algorithm is significantly weakened.

The manufacturing process: due to manufacturing tolerances, all the pins in the lock do not work simultaneously. In other words, with a certain tension applied to the locking mechanism, the tension on one pin exceeds the tension on others. Mathematically, this means it is possible to separate the key in our example into six separate keys with only six possible solutions for each. So with a proper tool, one need only make the try with no more than $6 \times 6 = 36$ combinations to open the lock. Though this attack may look simple, it does require certain skills and equipment.

Given the factors cited above, it should now be quite clear that the security of the lock in our example can be summarized as follows:

- The lock provides reasonable protection against a brute force attack, unless the value of the attack's success exceeds the relatively high cost of manufacturing of a large number of the keys and it is acceptable to the attacker to carry out a 65-hour attack.
- The lock within a master key system provides a shortcut for an attack that requires minimal skills and equipment, enabling the attacker to open all locks in such a system.
- The lock provides practically no protection against a reasonably skilled and equipped attacker.

From a cryptographic point of view, all these assumptions lead to two major approaches to carrying out an attack: first, try a brute force approach (by simply trying all possible combinations of the key), or second, find a shortcut that will effectively reveal some part of the key, effectively reducing its length and making the attack easier. Thus if, in the mechanical lock example above, a manufacturer specified that the height of any pin could not differ more than one value from adjacent pins, this would significantly reduce a number of possible combinations of the key and would diminish the effectiveness of the key.

When considering a brute force attack, the crypto robustness of the lock notwithstanding, the physical space involved in access security includes other practical factors: the risk of exposure while taking that much time in front of a door that does not belong to the attacker, the cost of manufacturing the keys, and even the sheer weight of the keys to bring to the lock. All these factors make a brute force attack of physical space access control systems impractical. A potential attacker might well be better off working for minimum wage rather than trying a brute force attack.

These are further typical questions that should be asked about an access security system:

- Is the algorithm known to the potential attacker? Usually it is, or at least it is relatively easily determined.
- Is the length of the key available to the potential attacker? Usually it is, often even published by the manufacturer.
- Can a key sample be available to the potential attacker? Often it can be.
- Can multiple keys be available to the potential attacker? Often they can be.
- What are the components of the implementation?

The last point, the components of the implementation, is probably the most important practical area that both offensive and defensive efforts concentrate on. By definition though, the defensive work is more difficult than the offensive. Defense has to cover all possible venues for an attack at all times, while the offense need only succeed in just one place at one time.

The process of implementation. Let us look at the process of implementation of the lock in the example. Access control systems typically require necessary manufacturing processes. These characteristics should be carefully considered in analysis of access control systems so the difference between these systems and data confidentiality systems is well understood and taken into consideration. These factors historically have led to different trends in the development of access control systems. To a large extent, due to the technological challenges of manufacturing, access control systems are liable to being compromised by shortcuts that circumvent their underlying theoretical algorithms. This in turn has led to introduction of the concept of "defense in depth."

2.3 Defense in Depth

If a king realized that he had a less-than-perfect lock on the door to his treasure vault, he could post a sentry at the entrance in addition to the lock on the door. This would make it difficult to have access to the lock long enough to defeat it. However, the king might realize that the sentries could have their own weaknesses, and one might conceivably grant access to the lock to a brother of his girlfriend. Then the king would have to introduce another layer of security. He might surround the door and the sentry with a double fence and have tigers roam through this corridor. This principle can be extended indefinitely, but the point is that access control systems are often vulnerable cryptographically—and even more vulnerable due to their implementation—so they have to have additional *independent* means of defense. These other means often take access control security to a different level.

Cost considerations are important, and often they are a dominant factor in many widely used systems. This means that the manufacturing tolerances of a lock that can be sold competitively are usually large enough to permit easy "picking" by a reasonably skilled person. Interestingly, improving tolerances of this type of a lock can actually lead to it being more easily defeated by other methods like "bumping" which, without getting into the details, involve a device that "shakes" all pins at the same time, making them move to the lock-opening position. This means that the lock's algorithm is inherently weakened significantly simply by the fact that it is manufactured.

The important point to be made about access control systems is that the implementation of a cryptographic algorithm cannot strengthen the algorithm. Furthermore, any cryptographic algorithm is weakened by its implementation. We will return to this point later in this book.

We have looked at the impact of manufacturing peculiarities in a mechanical lock. The issue is actually much broader. Weakness introduced by the manufacturing process is only one of many venues usually presented to an attacker by the implementation of a crypto algorithm.

The next vulnerable points in algorithm implementation are the sales, installation, and service channels. During those activities, the lock can be compromised by either copying the key or modifying the lock. Without going into a detailed description, the important point here is that it is practically not possible for a user to detect such a compromise. In other words, the user has no idea if any unauthorized copies of the key were made or if a lock has been modified to accommodate another key along with the regular one.

These inherent weaknesses of access control devices have led to the development of comprehensive security systems. A lock is an access control security mechanism. To provide a meaningful defense against a reasonably skilled and equipped attacker who knows how to address the venues of attack opened by implementation, one needs to develop a security system, i.e., the defense in depth mentioned above. In such systems, mechanical locks are complemented by security guards, identity verification, security alarms, etc. The preferred method is to provide an additional security system component that is independent of all others, so that a compromise of one component will not lead to the automatic compromising of others. For instance, a security guard checking the identities of people trying to access the door with the lock against the list of cleared personnel would be an additional security mechanism in the system. Another guard watching a CCTV monitor and making sure that a person opening the door does not look suspicious or unusual while opening the lock would be another security mechanism. However, it should be recognized that if these functions are performed by the same guard, these are not independent mechanisms, and overall security is not strengthened..

A defender has to be very methodical and thorough in analyzing the potential venues of attack. At the same time, a particularly hard challenge is that he may not recognize all the venues of an attack presented by the implementation of the algorithm. In the real world, this is exactly what often happens: an attacker's creative approach recognizes a new venue, one not previously used, and thus likely not addressed by the defender. Historically, attackers have displayed a significant level of creativity in finding such venues. Many of these venues were spectacular—the movie *How to Steal a Million* is a good example—and it is reasonable to suspect that only a small portion of successful attacks became known.

As a trend, military-style attacks and attacks related to theft of identifiable physical property are usually known. At the same time, attacks related to intelligence or intellectual property usually do not get publicity, even *if* detected. It was no accident that the KGB, well known for its extremely robust security measures, applied more effort to detecting an attack than to protecting against it, certainly regarding its most sensitive secrets. In fact, the detection of an attack of this nature should be considered a partial failure of the attack. Indeed, an attacker who is able to steal a battle plan of an opposing army is better off if his success is not known to the defender. At least not until after the battle is over.

As we noted above, one of the questions regarding implementation of a cryptographic algorithm is whether or not the implementation creates shortcuts to the algorithm itself, i.e., even without manufacturing issues. A classic example of this is the implementation of a master key system for a number of mechanical locks. A study by Matt Blaze of AT&T Labs (www.crypto.com/masterkey.html) shows that possession of one key of such multiple lock system (a hotel is a typical example) and access to just one lock creates a shortcut that enables an attacker with minimal general purpose equipment and no special skills to build a master key that can open any lock in the system. This can be done by trying no more than just 30 combinations. If we consider, say, 100 locks in a system with a master key, then, algorithmically it should represent $100 \times 46,656 = 4,665,600$ (strictly speaking $4,665,501$— if done by one attacker and previous results are considered) combinations to open all the locks in the system. By implementing the master key system, this number is reduced to just $6 \times 5 = 30$ combinations.

This returns us once again to one of the most important points in security. A cryptographic algorithm is always weakened by its practical implementation, usually significantly. Furthermore, while the algorithm itself is usually analyzed mathematically, the post-implementation device often is not. This, at the very least, leads to unrecognized risks.

Do all types of weakening of the cryptographic algorithm have the same effect? Apparently not.

Algorithm Degradation. A detailed look into implementation can reveal two distinctly different categories of algorithm degradation: manufacturing and practicality. This is an extremely important point in analyzing not just access security, but security in general.

Manufacturing limitations are unavoidable. They represent the limitations of technology of a given time. In other words, something can be either not possible to achieve given the current state of technology, or it can be economically unjustifiable.

Practicality is a totally different category. It entails something users are reluctant to do to achieve or enhance security. It can also be called "inconvenience." For instance, not having a master key for a company's offices is "impractical" or "inconvenient." Indeed, copies of all the offices' keys could be kept in a safe and retrieved as needed, and cleaning service people could be supervised by security personnel while cleaning offices. But this is inconvenient and usually termed impractical, despite the fact that the company usually has no control over cleaning personnel while giving them unsupervised access to the company offices with sensitive information inside, when only an easy prey of a lock and a will separates these outsiders from the organization's assets.

The conclusion here is very clear: security is provided not by a cryptographic algorithm, but by its implementation. Furthermore, implementation aspects must be analyzed separately and must consider both technological limitations and practical implementation choices.

Feedback. A final essential consideration is feedback. Feedback from an attempt on an access security system is probably the most overlooked aspect of access systems analysis. We often assume that feedback is available, i.e., that an attacker knows if an attempt has succeeded or not, and that he knows it instantly. In fact, these assumptions are not always valid. Getting feedback can be problematic for an attacker, and the time and effort involved can be major obstacle for an attack. Suppose, in our example of the lock, that one try by brute force attack takes 5 seconds. All the attempts would potentially require up to about 65 hours of a nonstop attack. Regardless of other factors, that could be a bit tiring.

To summarize the feedback issue, we need to know:

- Is feedback available?
- What is the time required to get feedback?
- What is the effort required to get feedback?

All the attacks described above rely on an immediate feedback from the attempt. The first absolutely necessary component of such feedback is the criterion of success. In a case of lock-picking, the intermediate criterion of success is the fact of the pin under pressure being released, i.e., the fact of finding the cut in the pin stack. This presents a binary situation: the pin cut is either found or not. If the cut is not found there is no point in continuing the attack because this pin would still keep the lock secured. The final criterion of success, of course, is the fact of the lock opening, also a binary situation. It may seem obvious that this binary situation is always available, but that may be not true, as we will see in the following chapters.

There are some approaches to finding a solution to a lock in which the attacker gets the lock to provide feedback like an "oracle." The attacker asks this "oracle" a limited number of questions, and the "oracle" gives away its secret by answering those questions. This approach utilizes feedback in a more sophisticated way.

Another component of necessary feedback is the time needed to receive such feedback. Calculating the time necessary for an attack is usually based on the number of tries necessary multiplied by the time necessary for each try. But this is not an accurate estimate, as it is based on the assumption that the intermediate feedback is instantaneous, which may or may not be true. A correct estimate of attack time should be based on the number of tries multiplied by the sum of the time required by the try, plus the time needed for feedback. We will return to this subject in later chapters.

In summary, we may conclude that the following components are necessary for a successful attack:

- Knowledge of the algorithm underlying the security system
- Knowledge of the structure of the key (length of the key and other parameters, preferably a sample of the key; access to multiple samples of the keys is the best)
- Specifics of the algorithm implementation (shortcuts introduced by technological limitations; shortcuts introduced by "practical" considerations)
- Access to the lock
- Intermediate feedback from the attack attempts
- Final feedback from the target
- Sufficient time for the attack so the number of necessary attempts multiplied by the sum of the attempt and the feedback is less than the time that can be afforded operationally

As we saw in the discussion of the pin tumbler lock, this device provides plenty of opportunities for easily cracking it. The access security industry's natural response was to develop the combination lock.

2.4 The Combination Lock

The initial idea was to deny an attacker the easy venue of using the keyhole for the attack. Naturally, the best way to do that was to get rid of the mechanical key and keyhole altogether. Generally, a combination lock is protected by a mechanism where several rings (often 3) have to be aligned in a specific manner for the lock to be opened. A common configuration is to use 3 rings that would be marked in numbers from 0 to 99. Cryptographically, this would give approximately: 100 X 100 X 100 = 1,000,000 combinations. Using a brute force approach with a specialized electro-mechanical tool that attempted one combination in 5 seconds in a lock shop would require up to 1,389 hours, or about 58 days. This is hardly acceptable for an average attacker.

So the algorithm seems to be sufficient, and the brute force approach is not operationally feasible.

However, the implementation of this algorithm opens some shortcuts. It is possible to manipulate this lock. For instance, the implementation usually includes a spring-loaded lever that falls into a slot in a metal wheel, and slots on every wheel come in contact with other parts while the wheel is turning. These events create vibrations that can be picked up by a good ear and easily by a good accelerometer. This will produce the key number on each wheel. The only remaining unknown would be which number belongs to which wheel. For a common lock with three wheels this would reduce the number of combinations to 6. A competent attacker would require access to the lock for only a few minutes, if that long.

So far this chapter has been concerned with mechanical locks, and we can sum up their security issues as follows:

- The level of entropy in the algorithm is usually sufficient, particularly considering the time required for one attempt (try) using a brute force approach.
- Implementation introduces shortcuts, undermining the robustness of the algorithm. These implementation short-cuts can be divided into two groups: manufacturing-introduced shortcuts and procedural shortcuts.
- The impact of shortcuts is so significant that cryptographic analysis of the lock is rarely done. Instead, designers have concentrated on counteracting the shortcuts, often creating further layers of defense and generally trying to make it difficult to approach the lock.
- The prevailing method of counteracting the shortcuts is making the approach to the lock (access to the lock) difficult for an unauthorized person. In high-end access security systems, this is usually successful.
- In all, designers of access control security systems are usually reasonably successful in making an attack on a mechanical lock a virtually symmetrical situation, i.e., the cost of attack is comparable to the potential benefit of success.

CHAPTER 3

ACCESS SECURITY—ELECTRONIC SYSTEMS

Now let us go one step further and review some electronic access systems, which are another class of physical space access control security systems.

The history of electronic locks is far shorter than the history of mechanical locks. However, there is a detectable pattern in this class of security systems. A functional block-diagram of a typical electronic access system is depicted in Fig. 3-1.

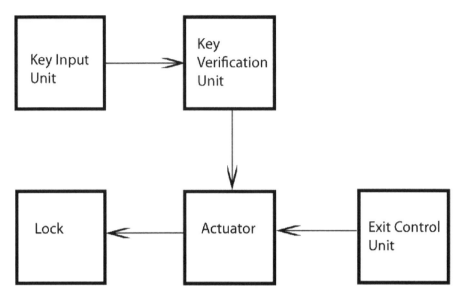

Fig. 3.1

3.1 System Components

Several parameters distinguish different types of electronic access systems. Usually these parameters reflect different types of the above-mentioned units, especially the key and key input unit. Thus:

- A key can be either a number to remember, a hardware device of some sort, or a physical parameter of a user such as a fingerprint or an eye retina image.
- A hardware key can be of a magnetic tape type or wireless, among others.
- A hardware key can be passive or active.
- A key input unit can be a passive or interrogator type.
- A key verification unit can be a simple comparison unit or it can be a computing device performing some algorithmic computation.

- An actuator can be a simple solenoid that moves the lock bolt or it can be a more complicated mechanism that moves several mechanical locking mechanisms upon a command from the key verification unit.
- An exit control unit can be just a push-button or a mass proximity sensor.

Now let us review the main components of electronic access control systems.

Despite these variations, there is a significant commonality among all electronic access control security systems. A key is introduced into a lock through an electromagnetic or optical process, whether it is a pressing of the keypad buttons, inserting a USB stick in a port, waving a proximity key near the sensor, or providing an optical input such as a fingerprint or retina image. In any of these cases, the result of the key application is an electric current flowing through the lock's circuitry. This current delivers the key parameters to the key verification unit. In other words, key application is transformed into an electric signal to the key verification unit. Then:

- The key signal delivered to the key verification unit is compared with the key stored there and the acceptance or rejection signal is generated in the unit.
- An acceptance/rejection signal is delivered to the key input unit display.
- The acceptance signal is delivered to the actuator as a command to open the lock.
- The actuator unlocks the lock, usually through a powerful electromagnetic action.
- The key input unit is usually placed in close proximity to the lock.

An exit unit, often a sensor or a button, is a response to "practical" considerations, mainly of fire hazard emergency. A mass exit of people needs to be expedited, and usually there is no time for dealing with security locks. In other words, security is suspended to ensure safe exit. Besides, it is considered redundant to require use of security to exit the facility. Often, exit is facilitated by a sensor that reacts to a certain mass (a person) approaching the door from inside toward the exit. This sensor generates a signal that employs the lock actuator, bypassing the key verification process. In older systems it was possible to manually open the lock from inside, for example by pressing a button, thus bypassing the key and controlling the actuator.

The next logical step is to examine if implementation shortcuts are introduced in this type of electronic security system and how they can be exploited.

- **Key Input Unit**. There are several commonly found types of key insertion unit:
- **Dial pad,** where a user dials a certain number (the key).
- **Magnetic tape reader**, where a user swipes the card with a strip of magnetic tape that has the key magnetically written there.
- **Proximity reader**, where a reader using an electromagnetic (EM) signal to interrogate a key with an electronic circuit and expects a certain EM response (the key).
- **Optical reader** that interrogates a certain image (a fingerprint or an eye retina) and expects to receive a certain image (the key).

Let us review the potential venues for an attack on these particular elements of an electronic lock.

Dial pad. The dial pad is the oldest type of key insertion unit, dating back well over half a century. Its advantage is that a user does not need to carry a physical key; the key is memorized by the user and dialed on the pad to gain access. There are several ways to attack a dial pad:

- An earlier method was based on the fact that the keys for these locks' 9-digit pads frequently contained 4 digits, and usually the digits are not repeated. This way, a theoretical level of entropy is

$$n!/(n\text{-}k)! = 3024.$$

By identifying which buttons are pressed by legitimate users an attacker can reduce it to k! = 24. This means that by just identifying "used" buttons an attacker can open the lock in less than just 25 attempts. Such identification can be done either simply by visual observation or by applying some sort of substance that is not visible in daylight but can be revealed by say, ultraviolet light.

- For ease of remembering, users often utilize a "geometric" key that is based on geometry of the key digits within the keypad. This practice simplifies the attack even further.

- An electromagnetic intercept can be utilized if a key combination is more complex or if identification of "popular" buttons is not possible. A simple EM receiver can intercept electric signals generated by dialing the key by legitimate users. Such a receiver can be either placed in the vicinity of the lock clandestinely, or it can be carried by an attacker at the time when a legitimate user dials the combination. Relatively simple subsequent analysis can produce the correct key for the lock.

Magnetic tape reader. Magnetic tape readers are very popular in access security systems. The unit reads data (the key) written on the strip of magnetic tape that is swiped through the unit's receiving slot, very similar to credit card swipes. The process generates an electric signal to the key verification unit that either accepts or rejects the reading. The key on the magnetic strip can be very long, providing an opportunity to create a significant level of entropy. At the same time, this device provides a lock shortcut. The most obvious weakness of this approach is that the key is exposed to be read. In fact, even with the least sophisticated set of equipment, such as a basic magnetic tape reader, an attacker can acquire a copy of the key if he can get hold of the key sample for a few seconds. When users carry their access cards with the magnetic strip key, it is usually difficult to have the card in sight and in full control all the time.

Proximity reader. A proximity reader is somewhat similar to the magnetic tape reader, except that the carrier of the key is an electronic circuit instead of a magnetic tape. This circuit is interrogated by the proximity reader with an EM signal, and it responds with an EM signal containing the key. If the response is correct, the lock is opened. While creating reasonable cryptographic entropy, this type of key entry device also creates significant opportunity for an attack. The interrogating signal from the reader can be intercepted and duplicated. For instance, an EM receiver planted in the vicinity of the reader or simply concealed during a legitimate entry can obtain a copy of the interrogating signal from a particular lock. Subsequent use of such a signal outside the facility, near a legitimate user carrying the key card (a nearby lunch deli or a bar could easily be used), will cause a response that contains the key. Duplicating that response signal at the lock would open it.

Optical reader. A fingerprint-based optical reader certainly can create significant entropy. However, besides its technological challenges, it also creates a significant shortcut. In fact, just by using the device, a legitimate user leaves a fingerprint on the receiving plate. This fingerprint can be relatively easily "lifted" off that plate and reproduced in a form that can be used as a copy of the key later. The newer type of the optical reader involves use of eye retina to be scanned by the key input device. It has the same level of advantages as the fingerprint-based system, but does not leave a "print" to duplicate. This makes it probably the most sophisticated key input device. Outside of scanning a legitimate user's retina, an attacker would be prompted to seek other venues for an attack rather than attacking the key and key input device.

Key Verification Unit. A key verification unit generally contains valid keys in its memory. It receives key input from the key input unit and compares it with the keys in its memory. If the introduced key is valid, the unit generates an "accept" signal to the actuator that leads to activating the lock opening mechanism. The obvious vulnerability within the unit itself is the possibility of corruption of the comparison software. While it is certainly possible to attack this software, operationally it is a relatively difficult task. It is easier to attack the signal from the key input unit to the key verification unit. As an electric signal, this can be generated from outside of the facility, but this also would require detailed knowledge of the system, relatively sophisticated equipment, and is only possible if the signal is conducted through a cable with poor EM shielding. These considerations make the key verification unit an unattractive target.

Actuator. The actuator receives a command signal from the key verification unit, manual access control button, or an exit sensor and operates the lock-opening mechanism, usually an electromagnet. The actuator can be influenced by an attacker emulating a command signal from either one of these sources. This command is usually very simple in structure and easily intercepted by an EM receiver, so that duplicating it often is not a technically difficult task. In addition to this, often a typical solenoid that actually moves the mechanical part of the lock can be attacked with a powerful electromagnet, thus simply opening the lock. Attacking an actuator is an ultimate shortcut in attacking the lock. It bypasses the entire security algorithm, no matter what the theoretical level of entropy, nor the sophistication level of the implementation.

The various attacks on electronic locks described above can be summarized as follows, but it should be noted that it is not necessary to attack all the components above. The attacker usually has the advantage in that he has to succeed in only one place, while the defender must cover all the venues. For instance, knowledge of actuator weaknesses may be sufficient because the attacker does not have to worry about any particulars of the key. So the list above can be reduced to the following basic list of the attack necessities, which would suffice for a successful attack:

- Access to the lock, and either of a sample of the key or via knowledge of the implementation
- Actuator-based shortcuts
- Key validation shortcuts, i.e., knowledge of the underlying algorithm and structure of the key
- Feedback from an attack attempt
- Sufficient time for attack implementation

Further analysis of this list shows that apart from a variable-specific method of an attack, there are three fixed requirements for a successful attack on an electronic lock:

- **Access to the lock**
- **Feedback from an attack attempt**
- **Sufficient time for implementing the attack**

3.2 Complex Approach to Access Security

The list above is fundamental for attacking a lock, whether it is mechanical or electronic. The conclusion from the discussion of physical locks is that they can be relatively easily penetrated. Designers of access control security systems usually know that, and they know they need to compensate for the shortcuts created by implementation of different access security algorithms in physical space. Furthermore, this compensation must come from an independent angle so it is not automatically compromised by the shortcuts. This is called a complex approach to access security.

The usual compensation comes in forms of monitoring systems and procedural security. Essentially, in order to achieve a reasonable security level we need to deal with the fundamental requirements for the attack listed above. We have to deny an attacker at least one of these three conditions. Let us take a look at these requirements:

- **Access to the lock.** Access to the lock can be controlled by different means, like posting a sentry who requires an ID from anyone accessing the lock. Another solution would be to use remote surveillance of the lock. A further solution is to post a sentry beyond the entry point, inside the facility, and ensure that the sentry knows every legitimate user personally. Security specialists have come up with a wide variety of measures that complement the security of the lock.
- **Feedback.** A sufficient level of entropy of the lock requires multiple attempts to penetrate it. If knowledge of the effect

of an attempt is not available, the next attempt is pointless. In other words, if we try to enter a key, we would not go further in our attack unless we knew whether that attempted key was correct or not. This point is very important in cyber security.

- **Sufficient time for implementing an attack.** As discussed before, the time for an attack should be calculated as a sum of attack attempts plus the time to receive feedbacks. For instance, if we know that it would take two seconds to dial a combination and one second to try the door if it opens, it would yield timing of about 3 seconds per try. If we know that an attacker would have 30 seconds of unimpeded access to the lock, it would allow him to make 10 attempts at the lock. With a 4-digit key on a 9-digit keypad, this would afford him about .07 percent chance of success. However, if the attacker identified the four digits used for the key, his chance of success would be about 42 percent.

These considerations lead to a fundamental strategy in developing access security systems:

- **Control access to the lock**
- **Limit time allowed at the lock**
- **Make feedback difficult**

It is possible to address these issues in physical space. We have a reasonable level of success with access security control systems in physical space due to the fact that we supplement physical locks with other measures in accordance with this strategy. This strategy has an interesting characteristic, in that it reverses the situation between the attacker and the defender: the defender has to succeed in denying the attacker just one of these conditions, but the attacker has to succeed in all three of them to achieve success. This balance is not valid, of course, if the attacker has a copy of the key and can comply with the procedural security.

PART II
CYBERSPACE

CHAPTER 4

CYBERSPACE—GENERAL

The word "cyberspace" (from "cybernetics" and "space") was coined by science fiction novelist and seminal cyberpunk author William Gibson in his 1982 story "Burning Chrome" and popularized by his 1984 novel Neuromancer. The portion of the latter cited in this respect is usually the following:

Cyberspace. A consensual hallucination experienced daily by billions of legitimate operators, in every nation, by children being taught mathematical concepts...A graphic representation of data abstracted from the banks of every computer in the human system. Unthinkable complexity. Lines of light ranged in the nonspace of the mind, clusters and constellations of data. Like city lights, receding.

Despite its originally negative overtone, the term no longer carries a negative connotation.

Gibson later commented on the origin of the term in the 2000 documentary "No Maps for These Territories": "All I knew about the word 'cyberspace' when I coined it, was that it seemed like an effective buzzword. It seemed evocative and essentially meaningless. It was suggestive of something, but had no real semantic meaning, even for me, as I saw it emerge on the page."

—From "Cyberspace" in Wikipedia, January 2012

Since the novelist William Gibson coined the term "cyberspace," it has become a commonly used term. Some people view it as a set of computers and the wires connecting them; others view it as a source of readily available inexpensive information; others view it as a marketing space designed to facilitate their sales and increase profits; and yet others apparently view it as a target-rich space for committing crimes with little risk of being caught and punished. Instinctively, by cyberspace we generally mean the same recently evolved phenomenon, but we often imply different aspects of it. This may be acceptable for a general discussion, but for more specific work in the security field we need more precision.

4.1 Categories of Spaces

Definition of a Space. It is difficult to define cyberspace without a definition of "a space." Numerous definitions of the word "space" have been used for a wide variety of applications. Since for the purposes of this book we need to study various aspects of both cyberspace and our physical world, i.e., physical space, and their interaction, we need at least a very general definition of a space. Thus:

- **A space is an entity that exists along and within its dimensions, with certain environmental conditions, where native objects exist and interact, processes take place, and some laws and rules are applied.**

But formulating a precise single definition of cyberspace is very difficult at this time when we are just beginning to understand the concept. What seems to be clear is that cyberspace is an information and communications space. Indeed, cyberspace is where information exists and is stored, processed, and communicated with certain laws and rules applied.

Let us explore some of the qualities and attributes of cyberspace, particularly those that are different from the physical world we are used to.

Generally, the nonkinetic interaction of objects in a space is conducted through channels of communication. While communications channels are not themselves part of the above definition of a space, we consider communications channels along with objects as the basic components of cyberspace.

- **Cyberspace communication channels are created by the interaction of physical space objects, and these physical space objects provide the infrastructure of cyberspace communications.**

Other channels of communications are possible but we do not understand their nature yet.

Properties of a Space. Any space has properties that can be categorized as follows:

- **Type**, i.e., whether it is material or abstract.
- **Limitativity**, i.e., whether the space's dimensions are limited or not (any space is limited to exist within its dimensions).
- **Continuity**, i.e., whether the space is continuous or not (this is related to whether all of its dimensions are continuous or not).
- **Homogeneity**, i.e., whether the space is homogeneous or not.
- **Contiguousness**, i.e., whether the space is contiguous or not. While this term is not conventionally used to categorize a space, it is probably the closest to the intended meaning. The reason for its introduction here is that this quality can be best observed in the Internet where parts of the Internet can be closed for technical or political reasons, effectively disconnecting these parts from the rest of the Internet.

This categorization of a space is not an attempt to categorize a space in all its scientific aspects. Rather, it represents only the categories that have a direct bearing on cyber security.

- **Our universe is a physical space and is categorized as material, unlimited, continuous, homogenous, and contiguous.**

Our world is definitely material; it contains matter, and our earthly world consists of matter. We can sense it with our sensors: we can see, hear, smell, and touch parts of it. Advancing technologies are enabling us to expand our ability to sense the world: we can use radar, X-ray, etc., to detect images of objects otherwise invisible to our naked eye in our world.

Our universe is unlimited; at least we have not found any evidence of its limits. Theoretically, there should be enough space in it for everyone without triggering conflicts. This notion, however, does not address the "location, location, location" issue that is applicable well beyond the real estate business. So the conflict-free concept may be problematic for humans even within an unlimited universe. But in real life at this time we do not yet have the means to utilize this quality of the universe, and so far for all practical purposes we are pretty much stuck with this planet Earth. The size of the Earth is **limited**, making our earthly physical space that we call world limited. Consequently, we have to deal with a wide range of real estate issues. This categorizes our world as limited, and this limitation plays a major practical role in our lives.

Our world is homogenous. This means that matter is the same everywhere, and all objects consist of the same elements (maybe in different compositions), and the same laws of physics are applicable in all parts of it. At least we have no indications to the contrary yet.

Our world is contiguous. Contiguousness is a term that needs special explanation. The question is whether we can exclude part of a space. In our world, we cannot effectively isolate any part of it. For instance, the Chinese Great Wall separated China from the rest of the world for a while, but China still continued to exist and still was a part of the world, albeit difficult to access. The wall did not affect matter as such inside China during the separation time, and all laws of physics acted unimpeded. Likewise, in a living or office space, all the parts are contiguous, i.e., they are connected. But we can put a wall in a space, separating one part of the space from another. In our physical world generally we cannot do that— the separated parts still remain parts of physical space, though for access purposes the space becomes noncontiguous. This has a direct bearing on cyberspace. For example, parts of the Internet can be disconnected, making it noncontiguous.

Thus when dealing with everyday issues within the limits of our planet, we find some of the characteristics of the universe as a space are of little consequence for our practical purposes.

- **We can categorize our Earth's physical space as material, limited, continuous homogenous, and contiguous. The most significant difference for our practical purposes is the limitation of size, and this plays a major role in our lives.**

Defining Cyberspace. Cyberspace is often equated with the Internet, or even a part of it such as the World Wide Web. However, it should be noted that cyberspace is a broader term than the Internet. Let us review characteristics of cyberspace so we can come up with objective and relevant parameters that will enable us to analyze this space.

We know that cyberspace is a man-made space; we actually built it. If we build something, usually there is a reason. Our overriding reason for building cyberspace was to achieve significant, qualitative improvements in the accumulation and dissemination of information that would satisfy our burgeoning informational needs. A significant factor here is that information is an asset. In fact, information has been traded for many centuries. Sometimes information has little value, and sometimes its value is crucial and paramount for our vital issues, including human life. Like any asset, information is tied to ownership, sometimes public, sometimes private. Information as property requires reliability and security as significant criteria in building cyberspace. We always want to protect our assets. Thus we can say that:

- **We built cyberspace to achieve significant improvements in accumulation, processing, and dissemination of information in a way that would satisfy our burgeoning informational needs in a reliable and secure way and assure that property rights are not violated.**

We will return to the security aspect of information in detail later. Given this practical definition and categorization of physical space, the next step is to categorize cyberspace. We know that cyberspace is a man-made space.

- **Cyberspace is Information and Communications space.**

It is important to realize that, from an informational stand-point, it does not matter whether information is stored on a flash drive or carved in a rock—what matters is the content; it does not matter whether information is transmitted over a laser beam or via the relay of a drum beat—what matters is whether the informa-tion is delivered from one object to another; it does not matter whether one uses his brain or his computer to analyze data—what matters is the algorithm used. So:

- **All systems that serve to store, process, and communicate information belong to cyberspace.**

Indeed, many earlier systems of processing information and communications existed for a long time, but they were designed for limited purposes. They did not really require consideration as a space. The trigger for specialized thinking about information and communications was the development of the Internet.

The development of the Internet was motivated by several major factors:

- The threat of a nuclear strike put communications of that time in jeopardy, thus prompting a need for survivability of wired communications systems.
- The rapidly growing need for fast transportation of large volumes of data between remote locations.
- The increasing need for expanding communications sys-tems required a more efficient switching technology than we had in our telephone systems.

These strategic needs led to the increased intensity in the search for an enabling technology, because the stated objectives were not achievable with the technology available at the time. The critical breakthrough was achieved by Paul Baran, who invented a new method of communications, the packet-switching technology, which became the enabling technological factor for building the Internet. This was followed by development of new communications protocols, which led to development of the Internet.

The rapid growth of the Internet necessitated a coherent look at the system, and that introduced the possibility of looking at it as a separate space. With further development and broader adoption of the Internet, we came to realization that it indeed represented a special space.

It is now clear that the concept of an information and communication space is broader than the Internet and may include some other entities or subspaces. If we view the Internet as a part of cyberspace, we can also apply the same criteria to describe other systems, such as the telephone system and the postal system. All of them should be viewed as subspaces of cyberspace. Indeed, all of them represent information and communications space. This broader concept of cyberspace can be particularly useful in the light of the continued trend of merging different communications technologies of the underlying infrastructures. Telephones, computers, and televisions are rapidly merging. Also, printed news media are rapidly evolving as content distribution through other information delivery means.

With this in mind, let us examine the categories of cyberspace in more detail, from a cyber security point of view.

4.2 Qualities and Categories of Cyberspace

One of the fundamental questions of cyberspace is: What kind of space is it? Is it abstract or material? This is a very important question.

An interesting fact about cyberspace is that, in a practical sense, its concept evolved after the development of the Internet. We tend to identify cyberspace with the Internet, or even with a part of it like the World Wide Web (the global network of web sites), but that is not correct. It is true that the concept of cyberspace became relevant only with development of the Internet. However, the main idea behind the development of the Internet was to improve the survivability and efficiency of the communications system that provides exchange of data among remote computers. Thus we sometimes tend to associate the Internet with electronics, because our experience with the implementation of the Internet is associated with computers, routers, switches, and electronic communications lines.

However, our real interest in cyberspace is informational, and electronics is just an implementation of our informational requirements.

The situation is similar to the relationship between the architecture and construction. Architects design structures for humans to live in, work in, etc., but the construction experts make a reality of the architectural solutions. So who controls and defines the process, the architects or the builders? Obviously, a significant interaction between the two professions is essential, but thousands of years of experience throughout history have shown that architecture has to be the driving force. With cyberspace, we are faced with a similar dilemma: what is the driving force in building cyberspace, the electronics or the requirements of information? From our user's standpoint, the most important criterion is what kind of information can we get, how well we can analyze it, what benefits we can derive from it, etc. What kind of computer we are going to use, or what kind of communications lines we need, are relatively less important. What is most important to us are the parameters of those benefits to us, not the implementation details, however relevant they may be to vendors of products who build the physical infrastructure of cyberspace. This suggests that our definition of cyberspace should be driven by informational aspects and not by the particulars of implementation.

Furthermore, if we chose to analyze cyberspace as an abstract space, we can utilize the large body of science with significant available mathematical tools. If, however, we chose to analyze cyberspace as a physical space, we will be forced to deal with the multitude of constantly changing electronic products, trying to mate them in a single system. Then when we look for guidance for what is needed either from market research or from the expressed "needs" of users, the analysis of these implementations will instead be mainly geared to the functionality and efficiency of the electronics. This approach does not address the informational nature of cyberspace but leads to poorly guided, and often chaotic, developments of different and not necessarily compatible products.

These considerations lead to a very important conclusion:

- **We should analyze the needs of cyberspace independently of their electronic implementations, and only then should we pass the implementational requirements on for the development of the relevant electronics.**

Needless to say, certain interactions and reality considerations have to be taken into account. For the most practical interaction between the industries involved, and their associated economic and political criteria, this dilemma should not be perceived as "what is more important," leading to rivalry between the two fields. It should be considered according to "what is the primary guiding force," which in turn should lead toward closer cooperation between the two fields. This quick analysis suggests that from both scientific and practical viewpoints, we can utilize math-based analytical methods to study cyberspace and deal with it as a space in a coherent manner to address our informational needs. This leads us to state that:

- **Cyberspace is an abstract space implemented on physical infrastructure**.

Does Cyberspace Have Limits? The next topic of interest is the **limitativity** of cyberspace. There are two distinctly different aspects of limitativity. One is the question whether dimensions are limited, and the other is whether the number of dimensions in cyberspace is limited.

Since we built cyberspace, we generally control the number of dimensions in it. For instance, in our postal system usually we have seven dimensions:

- Country
- State (province, or something like that)
- City
- Street
- Street number
- Apartment number
- Name

Some variations exist, but they are usually associated with efficiency of delivery, not with the fact of it. Each of these dimensions exists independently of others. For instance, it could be that different countries have the towns with the same name. Different towns can have the same street name. In other words, knowing all coordinates of an object (recipient) in a postal system means we can singularly identify this object's location in postal subspace of cyberspace. It should be noted that the zip code is not a structural dimension of the postal system; it is just an efficiency factor. In fact, it is possible to deliver a letter precisely to the address without knowing the zip code. From a cyberspace coordinates standpoint, it is a redundant parameter.

Can we increase the number of dimensions in cyberspace? The answer is clearly yes. We can add another .*something* to the Internet. We can also add another dimension in the postal address if needed, something like "John Smith XXI" (this system was common for some time, particularly within one social group, but became less fashionable after the French stopped the tradition in a pretty radical way by beheading Louis XVI).

Another question to be asked here is whether dimensions in cyberspace are limited. Conceptually, no, they are not limited. For instance, we can make our telephone system based on any number of digits, say 24. In yet another example, IPv4 Internet protocol allocates 32 bits for the IP address, theoretically giving us 2^{32} addresses. When we needed a greater range of addresses, IPv6 was developed with 128 bits allocated for the IP address, giving us 2^{128} addresses. If the need arises, we can allocate any number that we find appropriate. Similarly, early telephone systems were based on a small number of connected points, often requiring a telephone number of 4 digits. Later the telephone number was expanded to 10 digits in a single country, and we can expand the number further if we need it.

The word "conceptually" is very important in these examples, illustrating the point about cyberspace being abstract space. If we had defined cyberspace with electronic or some other physical implementations in mind, the answer could well have been: yes, because we have limitations in technology. Or it is too expensive to implement. So this is another confirmation that cyberspace is an abstract space. This leads us to the conclusion that:

- **Cyberspace has no natural limits both in the number of dimensions and in the size of its dimensions.**

Is Cyberspace Continuous? The next point to explore is **continuity**. We know that our physical space is continuous. Let us consider two points in this space. No matter how close we choose them, there is at least another point belonging to the same space that will fit between our two points. Let us examine cyberspace from this perspective.

In the Internet a location of a computer in cyberspace is determined by its IP address, expressed as xxx.xxx.xxx.xxx. Suppose we have two computers with the closest possible IP addresses such as: xxx.xxx.xxx.xx2 and xxx.xxx.xxx.xx3. We cannot locate them any closer in cyberspace, and there is no space for another computer between them, i.e., there is no such an IP address as xxx.xxx.xx2.5.

Similarly, in our telephone system there is no space for another telephone number between (xxx)-xxx-xxx2 and (xxx)-xxx-xxx3.

This trait is traceable through all the subspaces of cyberspace. For example, our postal address is discrete because normally there is no such public address as "Apartment 25.6."

These examples show that cyberspace is discrete, i.e., noncontinuous, even within its subspaces. So:

- **Cyberspace is noncontinuous.**

Is Cyberspace Homogenous? The next question to address is homogeneity of cyberspace. We have built more than one system that serves our information and communications needs. For instance, our postal and telephone systems serve the same purpose of addressing our informational needs. Should we view them as cyberspace?

The telephone system essentially serves the same purpose as cyberspace. It addresses informational needs of users. The telephone system uses a different technological base, i.e., circuit-switching technology as opposed to the packet-switching technology of the Internet, but in principle it complies with all other criteria for cyberspace, once again confirming our conclusion that cyberspace should be classified as an abstract space. This point is reinforced by the development of the Voice-over-IP technology that merges elements of the telephone system and the Internet. The trend toward the merging of these technologies sets new requirements for the infrastructural requirements of cyberspace. Thus, we can reasonably confirm that the telephone system is a part of cyberspace.

While a postal system uses a different physical structure, it still serves the purpose of transporting pieces of information such as letters from one user of the system to another. So, while predating cyberspace as we know it by a few centuries, in principle it shares the same definition of cyberspace. A notable difference, though, is that the postal system also transports physical objects that cannot be viewed as data and may bear no informational value. Should that be regarded as a disqualifier? That transportation of nondata objects is a parallel use of the physical infrastructure of the postal system. It represents a very practical optimization of the use of its physical infrastructure. Furthermore, it can also be viewed as an original technological limitation of the informational system. Indeed, all data and information originally were transported on a physical medium such as paper, wood, animal skins, human bodies, etc. In fact, a piece of paper is no more material than an electric current that transports an Internet packet from one point to another. Altogether, it is logical to conclude that the postal system is also a part of cyberspace. These reviews of the telephone and postal systems lead us to conclude that:

- **Cyberspace is generally inhomogeneous.**

However, this conclusion is only pertinent to cyberspace as a whole. At the same time, an important feature of every subspace is that it has to be homogenous, so that objects can easily "find" and communicate with each other. For instance, information sent via a letter cannot directly reach a recipient who is on an uninhabited island with only a satellite connection to the Internet. At the same time, communications are normally provided within a particular subspace, such as the postal system or the Internet. This leads us to the conclusion that:

- **Cyberspace consists of homogeneous subspaces.**

Is Cyberspace Contiguous? The next in this series of fundamental questions is whether cyberspace is contiguous. On the one hand, objects in cyberspace need to communicate with each other. This makes their contiguousness a virtual requirement.

On the other hand, for example, parts of the Internet can be temporarily disconnected, or destroyed altogether, disrupting the Internet's contiguousness. Also, some parts of the Internet can be separated by partitions, creating private networks with intermittent and conditional connectivity to the Internet itself. This is a complicated subject and will be addressed separately. However, for the purposes we have discussed so far we can reasonably conclude that the answer probably is that it may or may not be contiguous. So, for practical considerations let us conclude that:

- **Cyberspace is generally noncontiguous, with a contiguous core and intermittently contiguous parts** that can become a part of the contiguous space, depending on time or other variables, such as human decisions or technical infrastructure malfunctions.

The following table compares five major criteria of our physical space on Earth and cyberspace:

PHYSICAL SPACE on EARTH	CYBERSPACE
Material	Abstract
Limited	Has no natural limits
Continuous	Noncontinuous
Homogenous	Generally inhomogenous
Contiguous	Generally noncontiguous

The table shows that the two spaces are fundamentally very different. This means we have to be very careful when we apply our experience in one space to another kind of space.

CHAPTER 5

THE CYBERSPACE ENVIRONMENT

5.1 Structure of Cyberspace

Let us examine the structure of cyberspace. As we discussed previously, cyberspace is a space where native objects exist, processes take place, and certain laws and rules govern. This also means that its environment is conducive to certain native processes, such as communications, i.e., the transportation of units of data from one object to another.

To contain these objects, enable processes, and to implement its laws and rules, a space needs an appropriate set of dimensions. Accordingly, cyberspace has its dimensions, but since cyberspace is a nonhomogenous space, its different subspaces may have different kinds and numbers of dimensions. We build those subspaces for some specific purpose and determine their structures and their dimensions.

A structure of dimensions in a space represents its system of coordinates, thus:

- A position of a point relative to a particular dimension is called its coordinate in this particular dimension.
- A position of a point in a space is determined by a set of its coordinates in the dimensions comprising the structure of the space.
- A set of cyber coordinates of an object that involves its coordinates in every dimension of its subspace singularly determines this object's position in cyberspace.
- A full set of a cyber object's coordinates represents its cyber identity.

Cyberspace was conceived as a public information and communications space. This means that in order for data to be successfully transported from one object to another, an object's cyber identity has to be unique in cyberspace. At the same time, we have to recognize that objects are independent (as far as cyberspace is concerned, i.e., cyber-independent), and the number of dimensions in cyberspace is not limited. This means that an object is free to establish its own private space with any dimensions that may be advantageous for its intended functionality. These dimensions would not be visible from outside of the object unless communicated to other objects privately. In other words, cyberspace consists of public space known to all participants as well as private domains that may exist within cyber objects. An example of that could be a computer with an IP identity that contains its own proprietary system of computer files and private programs. These files and programs are cyber objects themselves, but are not publicly known to other cyber objects, so they publicly do not exist. However, a related computer with the knowledge of this private directory can address these objects. We will return to this aspect of cyberspace later.

Another peculiarity that we mention now and examine in some detail later is the temporary nature of cyber identity. Cyber identity essentially is a location in cyberspace. Once this point in cyberspace has been assigned to a particular user, the user has control over what object to locate there. In other words, it could be one computer at a certain point in time and another one sometime later. Actually, it would probably be more accurate to call it a public cyber identity. Unless otherwise noted, let us agree to call it simply a cyber identity. We will address the important and very practical subject of cyber identity later, in the cyber security part of this book.

These observations lead to an important conclusion:

- **Cyber identity (i.e., public cyber identity) is a full set of public cyber coordinates of an object in cyberspace.**

Unlike objects in much of our physical space:

- **Objects in cyberspace can have multiple legal cyber identities.**

If more than one object has the same cyber identity, it would create ambiguity and inhibit communications with those objects. Thus:

- **Any location in cyber space cannot be occupied by more than one object; a cyber identity is unique.**

5.2 The Environment of Cyberspace

As we discussed earlier, the environment of cyberspace has to be conducive to the processes taking place and to making it possible to implement and enforce cyberspace laws and rules. In other words, the cyberspace environment has to facilitate communications among the cyber objects, within its laws and rules.

In our physical space, we are accustomed to the fact that every object has a certain size. In other words, every object occupies a certain set of physical space coordinates that involves more than one point in every dimension. Very differently,

- **A cyber object has no size.**

A computer, however large in physical space, does not have any size as an object in cyberspace. It occupies only one point represented by a set of its cyber coordinates (e.g., an IP address). If a computer has more than one IP address, it simply acts as two different cyber objects, but it does not increase its size.

Single and Multiple Objects in Cyberspace. It is important to note that these considerations are pertinent only to singular cyber objects. An interesting situation is when a cyber entity consists of multiple objects. For instance, let us take a look at a network. Usually it consists of multiple computers. Together, they occupy a certain number of cyber locations, which may be viewed as a cyber area. This may be interpreted as a complex object consisting of simple objects. However, it seems more reasonable to call such an entity something like a cluster of objects rather than an object. Otherwise it would be very difficult to classify such clusters because their formation is not caused by cyberspace considerations, but rather by political, economic, military, etc., considerations generated outside of cyberspace.

An interesting scenario develops if we decide to make one of the dimensions in cyberspace reflect the amount of information contained within a cyber object, i.e., we add a data dimension to the cyberspace. For instance, suppose that a cyber object is a computer connected to the Internet. This computer occupies a single point of cyberspace with an appropriate set of cyber coordinates. The additional coordinate would be the amount of data in that computer's memory. The amount of data in that computer would be represented by the value of the data dimension, i.e., a single point in that dimension. This is very different from the physical memory of that computer, which would occupy a certain number of data cells, representing a volume of a certain size. This means that in cyberspace, if we choose to utilize a data dimension, an amount of data contained in a cyber object is represented by the location of an appropriate point on that dimension axis, but this does not seem feasible with high dynamics of data in a computer.

In our physical space, we are used to always having some distance between locations or objects. In many instances, this distance plays a major role in our decision-making. Very differently, there is no distance as such in cyberspace. Indeed, how would we determine a distance between two objects in cyberspace? The difference is only in the numbers of their cyber coordinates, while the physical distance between associated computers could vary from a few inches to thousands of miles. Thus

- **There is no concept of distance in cyberspace.**

Going further down the list of what we are accustomed to in physical space, we come to the subject of speed. Speed, in its many applications, usually is a measure of some process's progress. In the broad sense of mechanical implications, we usually associate it with progress of travel from one location to another, so that speed is usually proportional to distance traveled. However, there is no such thing as distance in cyberspace. Thus

- **There is no concept of speed in cyberspace.**

In our physical space, we constantly deal with energy fields such as electric, magnetic, and gravitational. However, these fields do not exist in cyberspace. Thus, it is important to note that:

- **There is no concept of energy is cyberspace.**

Consequently,

- **There are no gravitational, electric, or magnetic fields in cyber space.**

In our physical space, we deal with force all the time. Related to the previous point, it is important to note that there is no such thing as force in cyberspace. Thus

- **There is no concept of force in cyberspace.**

The further implication of the last observation is that:

- **There can be no mechanical impact in cyberspace.**

An important implication of these last several points is the difference between travel in physical space and travel in cyberspace. We all know that in physical space travel is relatively difficult (particularly during holiday times—there are no holidays in cyberspace either!) and expensive. However, in cyberspace we have the following advantages:

There is no friction and no distance, so it is inexpensive if not free; there is no airline or TSA, so there is no harassment in travel; and traffic jams are infrequent and can be mitigated with much less expenditure than required for fixing our roads. So we can say that:

- **Changing the location of an object (i.e., travel) in cyberspace is easy and almost free.** (Nothing is totally free, really.)

Visibility in Cyberspace. We are used to seeing objects in physical space. We know that in the most common experience, visibility is related either to emanating or to reflecting electromagnetic energy by an object. (Acoustic or hydro-acoustic "visibility" is a closely related concept). That emanated or reflected energy is registered by our sensors, thus establishing visibility. Furthermore, the emanation and reflection of energy by objects in physical space is involuntary, i.e., every object on earth emanates and reflects energy, regardless of our wishes. Sometimes we can somewhat control the emanations and reflections, but we cannot stop them. The only known exception here is the dark matter, which neither emanates nor reflects electromagnetic energy. However, we do not deal with the dark matter every day, or if we do, we do not know it.

Radically different, like dark matter in physical world, cyber objects in cyberspace do not emanate or reflect energy. Cyber visibility is established only by a deliberate request by one object and the voluntary response by another. In other words, if one computer wants to interact with another, it sends a proper request. The other computer replies to that request, and the reply is voluntary. This concept is true for all subspaces of cyberspace. For instance, if a person wants to establish a letter-based communication with another, he sends a letter to an appropriate address. The recipient has a choice of whether to reply or not, i.e., to be letter-visible or remain letter-invisible. The conclusion is that visibility in physical space is mandatory while in cyberspace visibility is voluntary. It should be noted that services such as requiring a recipient's signature (proof of delivery) are legal services, not cyberspace services. At the same time, a service like a notification of delivery by a carrier is a cyber service that fulfills communications reliability requirements of cyberspace. But neither of these types of services are structural parts of cyberspace.

- **Visibility in cyberspace is voluntary. In other words, a cyber object that has been addressed has a choice of becoming cyber-visible or to remain cyber-invisible.**

Let us summarize environment and peculiarities of cyberspace.

	CYBERSPACE	PHYSICAL SPACE
SPACE LIMIT	Not limited	Limited
OBJECT SIZE	NO	YES
MULTIPLE IDENTITIES	YES	Generally illegal
DISTANCE	NO	YES
GRAVITY	NO	YES
TRAVEL (Change of Location)	Easy, free	Difficult, expensive
VISIBILITY	Voluntary	Natural, unavoidable

5.3 Cyberspace Laws and Rules

There are two general categories of law: spatial and societal. Spatial laws are native to the space; objects in a space can discover them, but cannot change them. Newtonian laws of motion are an example of spatial laws in our physical space. Newton discovered them, but humans as objects in our physical space cannot change them. Further discoveries in physics resulted in deeper understanding of our space and its laws, but these were new discoveries, not a change in the law. For instance, Einstein discovered deeper relationships in our space, but it was a process of discovery, not a process that modified the Newtonian laws of motion. Effectively, for any law to exist it has to be enforced within its jurisdiction. Spatial laws are enforced by the nature of the space itself, and this enforcement is actually what makes them laws.

Societal laws are fundamentally different. They are made, changed, obeyed, disobeyed, and canceled—all by humans. In other words, they are not native to the space, but are relative, reflecting current understanding of "good," "evil," or "necessary" by a group of people who have enough power to make and enforce these laws. What is important here is that these laws are nonuniversal—they only relate to our own. For instance, in some societies, the law requires the killing of humans under certain circumstances, and in others it is against the law. Thus, these laws operate in certain jurisdictions. This concept is very important to our understanding and utilization of cyberspace.

Native Laws in Cyberspace. In order for a law to be real it has to be issued by an authority for an entire jurisdiction, and it has to be enforced in the entire jurisdiction. No entity has jurisdiction over entire cyberspace, i.e., there is no overall authority in cyberspace. Furthermore, no entity has jurisdiction even over a subspace such as the Internet or the international postal system. Thus, **societal or relative laws cannot effectively exist in cyberspace. This means that any attempt to make a relative law for cyberspace is futile.** For instance, suppose country A enacts a law that makes it illegal to communicate with any cyber object in country B. This is hardly an enforceable law. For instance, an object in country B can have a related object in a neutral country C. This way, this object in country B can communicate with objects in country A through its related object, with a low probability of detection in cyberspace. Thus this law can be enforced in country A with some chance of success through its government's means in physical space, but not in cyberspace. This means that any attempt to create societal laws relative to objects in cyberspace is essentially futile.

This leaves cyberspace with native or spatial laws. These laws may be described as follows:

- **Information is free to exist in cyberspace.**
- **Information cannot be destroyed. One can destroy a copy of information, but not information! This is one of the fundamental spatial laws of cyberspace.**
- **An object must have a cyber identity in order to exist in cyberspace.**
- **An object's cyber identity is unique, but is valid only for the moment.**
- **There are no spatial limitations on data exchange between cyber objects.**
- **There are no spatial limitations on data and content of data (i.e., information) in cyberspace.**

Rules in Cyberspace. Now let us take a look at rules in cyberspace. The general distinction between a law and a rule is sometimes hard to pinpoint. In a democratic society it is easy: the laws are made by democratically elected bodies, often for the benefit of the people, and rules are made by bureaucrats to bend the laws in favor of their own interests. A practical distinction might be: if you break a rule, you pay a fine; if you break a law, you go to jail. In other societies, the difference is not that clear. But while generally plausible, these descriptions are not very useful for scientific and technical purposes.

Rules are usually developed to prevent unwanted interaction between objects and to deal with interference in processes. In other words, rules are supposed to make a plurality of processes proceed in a more or less orderly manner, avoiding major collisions. Rules are often based on an authority's previous experience with more or less similar processes, and they supposedly reflect an attempt to improve processes. Also, rules are usually based on the current level of technology for an underlying process. For instance, at the time when only simplex communications were technologically available, the rule for using a communication line use was that you could either receive or transmit, but not both.

Similarly now, most rules in the Internet are based on the current technological limitations of its electronic infrastructure. As far as cyberspace is concerned, it simply means that these rules are reflected in parameters of cyber processes and can be described as process limitations. Usually communications rules are embedded in communications protocols.

5.4 Interaction Between Subspaces

Cyberspace is a communications space. All communications are based on common languages developed for the purpose. This necessitates utilization of common communication protocols that fulfill the role of common languages. For instance, the Internet Protocol (IP) makes it possible for computers to communicate over the Internet. Different protocols have been developed, usually for optimization of communications in one respect or another. Let us review a situation in which communication is required between two objects belonging to different subspaces. Let us suppose that these two subspaces consist of totally different dimensions. The two objects cannot "see" each other because they are not equipped to operate in another subspace. Furthermore, they are not equipped to comply with the other subspace's protocols. The situation is not conducive for communications. The solution is to create an avatar of an object in another subspace (or another space, for that matter). Such an avatar would serve as a translator between two subspaces and represent its object to another subspace generally.

For example, Mr. A wants to send a message to his son Mr. B, but A lives in a remote village with no electricity and its communications system consists only of a mailman visiting on horseback once a week. B, a renowned global-warming scientist, is in Antarctica on a scientific expedition, where mail service is far less frequent, but he has access to the Internet through a satellite connection. One communication solution is that A can send a letter to a friend C who lives in New York and has the luxury of both mail service and the Internet service. So, A sends the letter to C and asks to relay it to B. C receives the letter, scans it on his scanner, and sends it to B via e-mail. What happened here is that the information (the letter content) was transferred from one cyber subspace (mail) into another (Internet) with a "translation" from one protocol to another. In this case, C's computer with a scanner served as an avatar of A in the Internet subspace (the participation of C himself is not essential and can be automated).

Another example of this situation is a Voice-over-IP approach. In its embryonic form, a computer serves as an avatar of a user in an Internet subspace. It translates the acoustic signal of a user's voice into an IP-compatible format. These data are transmitted to a reciprocal computer that translates them into an acoustic signal to another user, the intended recipient of the signal. This arrangement serves as a physical space/cyberspace/physical space conduit. Further development has made this arrangement more interesting. The premise is that one of the communicating users does not have access to the Internet, but has access to the telephone system, i.e., another subspace of cyberspace. This requires transmission of data between the telephone system and Internet, i.e., two subspaces of cyberspace. The second computer has to translate the data from the IP-based protocol to a telephone system protocol, serving as the Internet avatar in the telephonic subspace. This led to the VoIP approach using the following path: physical space/cyberspace (Internet)/cyberspace (telephonic)/physical space.

These observations lead us to conclude that:

- **Communications between two spaces or subspaces require utilization of avatars addressing dissimilar dimensions and different communications protocols.**

- **Communications between two subspaces of cyberspace require utilizations of avatars addressing dissimilar dimensions and translating protocols of the two subspaces.**

5.5 Data vs. Information

Cyberspace is an information and communications space. The meaning of the word "information" here is rather general. For many applications, we tend to differentiate between **Data** and **Information**, but this differentiation is sometimes blurred, and that may lead to unnecessary confusion. It makes sense to make the difference more definitive. It looks logical to say that we take data in consideration but usually act on information. If we follow this logic, we discover that among numerous, usually rather casual references to the difference, the one that makes sense in cyberspace is

- **Data is a set of primitive factual elements.**
- **Information is meaningfully processed data.**

While logical questions like what is "primitive" and what is "meaningful" are likely to be asked, these definitions at least can serve reasonably well for practical purposes, though in an academic sense they admittedly are open for discussion.

It should be noted that communications systems do not, and should not, attempt to understand the contents of what they are transmitting and receiving, so for them everything transitioning through is data. This is different for the objects that are the recipients of communications.

- **Communications systems need not understand the contents of what they are transmitting and receiving, so for them everything transitioning through is data**.

For example, suppose some process control system measures some parameter, say speed. The measurements are quite meaningless until some analytical agent determines that the speed is too high, too low, or normal. In this case, the speed measurements are data, and the conclusion (based on the data processed in conjunction with some other data or information) becomes information. This illustrates the point that:

- **Information can usually become a reason for an action, while data usually cannot.**

This process, however, is not single-stage. After processing, data at some level becomes information; this information can become data for the next, higher-level stage.

For example, John is driving a car. His speedometer shows 70 miles per hour. This is data. Then John recalls that the speed limit on this highway is 55. Taken together and analyzed, it becomes information, i.e., having processed the data, John knows he is speeding. However, he does not see any police and decides he is reasonably safe on an open, wide highway with light traffic. The fact of his speeding becomes data. He goes on and, some time later, just when he reaches the top of a hill, he sees a police car down the hill on the shoulder. This is data. Taken together and analyzed, his speeding and the sight of the police car become information. The information is that he is in trouble. There's not much he can do at this point, and this information becomes data while he is going down the hill, slowing down, and preparing to stop after being pulled over by the police. While passing the police car, he notices that the policeman in the car is eating his hamburger. This is data. Having passed the police car, John sees no flashing lights in his rearview mirror. This is also data. Taken together with the fact of his speeding, it becomes information. Now John understands that he is lucky to get away with speeding this time. Then the fact of his luck becomes data. All of a sudden, John recalls that the police are often work in pairs, being within a mile or two from each other. This is data. Taken together with the fact that he was about to resume his 70-mile-per-hour speed and analyzed, it becomes information. John realizes that his chances of being caught speeding are higher than his tolerance for risk, and he decides to drive within the speed limit.

However, conventional use by most people suggests that generally users are interested in information while communications devices are concerned with data. With these considerations in mind, we are going to use the term **information** when content may be relevant and should be considered, and use the term **data** when it is not.

5.6 Summary of Interaction Between Cyber Subspaces

The dimensions of a space determine its system of coordinates. This aspect tells us that cyberspace is multidimensional in more than a conventional sense. Indeed, we can have two subspaces with two distinctly different sets of dimensions. And dimensions in cyber subspaces can be very different from another. For instance, the world telephone infrastructure is another subspace in cyberspace with its own set of dimensions and thus its own cyber coordinates. This means that if an object in one subspace wants to communicate with an object in another, they need a translator.

Furthermore, the object of one subspace may or may not be recognized as an object in another subspace. This means that an object in one subspace may need a "proxy" or an "avatar" in another subspace. For example, a letter sent through the mail is viewed by the postal service as a piece of paper to be delivered from address A to address B. However, as far as cyberspace is concerned, and the user as well, it may be a piece of information and the paper aspect of it may be of little relevance (unless the user is a lawyer, of course). Furthermore, if a user wants to send this information over the Internet, the letter has to be transformed from one subspace to another, i.e., it needs its cyber avatar. So we can say that:

- **Representation of objects of one cyber subspace in another may require an avatar.**

Interaction between different cyber subspaces can be complicated. Two different cyber subspaces may have some identical dimensions. For example, a modern cell phone has some of its cyber coordinates identical with the Internet so it can receive e-mail. At the same time, it has a different set of coordinates for telephone communications. In this case, only a part of an object in one cyber subspace can be recognized as an object in another subspace.

5.7 Distance and Latency

In physical space, distance is usually understood as the amount of separation between two points with certain coordinates in space. In cyberspace, coordinates are such parameters as an IP address. In this case "distance" does not have a meaning because it cannot reflect a degree of separation of one IP address over another. The interesting correlation to physical space is that the physical distance between any two computers does exist, but it also losing direct relevance because by the very nature of the Internet, a packet can travel from computer A to computer B by many different routes, and thus travel time can vary.

Furthermore, what is really important in communications, computers, and control systems is not the distance but latency, i.e., the time required for a batch of data to get from computer A to computer B. Latency in cyberspace is a function of many variables, but it has at least one constant component: the minimal latency required for an electromagnetic signal to travel the physical distance. The maximum realistic distance between two points on Earth does not exceed about 40,000 km, so that would require a theoretical latency of about 133 milliseconds. The remaining latency is induced by the physical infrastructure of cyberspace. Keeping in mind that cyberspace is an abstract space, latency should be treated as a parameter of the communication process.

Our physical space is commonly represented by three dimensions. "Length" is applicable to the three dimensions as the distance between points in the space. It means that, at least within this planet, space is limited. In other words, the more space is taken up by objects, the less is left for movement (travel). In cyberspace, the situation is quite different: first of all, the dimensions are not limited; secondly, an object does not have a size. So:

- The time to travel for an object is determined not by the distance between the two points but by the parameters of the communications process, such as the latency.

CHAPTER 6

CONTENTS OF CYBERSPACE

6.1 Objects in Cyberspace

The question of what constitutes a cyberspace object is a very interesting topic in itself. From the definition of cyberspace in the last chapter it is clear that the units of data and information are objects. Data files and information files are both cyberspace objects. Further analysis brings classes of such objects into focus. A computer file, such as a document file, can be passive. But it can also be active, like a computer program. Running a program is a cyber process. Thus we can categorize cyber objects as active cyber objects and passive cyber objects. Then we can further categorize cyber objects in the following way:

- **Passive cyber objects cannot initiate or run a cyber process.**
- **Active cyber objects can initiate and/or run a cyber process.**

Cyber objects can be regular objects (independent) or service objects. The main difference is that service objects exist only as part of cyberspace infrastructure. Examples of such objects are those that represent Internet routers and switches in cyberspace, i.e., their cyber avatars. They do not represent cyberspace users, but rather are subordinate to entities that maintain and manage the physical infrastructure of the Internet. They can be viewed as algorithmic descriptions of the corresponding devices' functionality, so we can see what function a particular service object performs on data traveling in cyberspace from one independent object to another.

Keeping in mind the main focus of this book, we will use the term "object" or "cyber object" when we mean independent cyber object. The study of service objects is a separate topic that is of a particular interest to communications entities and will be addressed later.

As we mentioned before, a challenging dilemma is whether or not to limit this class to abstract objects, such as data and information units. From an abstract perspective this approach would make the situation "cleaner" and easier to analyze. On the other hand, if we include another class of objects, such as hardware devices, that would make analysis more challenging. Indeed, computers are carriers of information. Data and information reside in computers. From an informational perspective it does not matter what is the carrier of the information, i.e., only the information itself is important. On the other hand, computers are a venue for attacks, and thus are important from security standpoint.

6.2 Cyberspace Infrastructure

This brings the whole class of cyberspace infrastructure into the focus. On the one hand, communications between the objects of cyberspace can be viewed abstractly as streams of data, making communication lines simply abstract channels of information. On the other hand, the functioning of cyberspace infrastructure is what actually keeps cyberspace together in the first place. While from an academic standpoint it is tempting to limit cyberspace to abstract objects, from a hardware-manufacturing standpoint it is probably advantageous to include cyberspace infrastructure with all its hardware elements in the picture. A challenging aspect of this approach is that some objects can have "dual citizenship," i.e., be part of two different spaces. For instance, a computer can be a cyber object, but at the same time it is clearly an object in physical space. Another daunting question: if someone strikes an Internet-connected computer with a large hammer and destroys its functionality, would that be a cyber attack or a physical attack? We can continue with these kinds of questions, increasing the complexity of the dilemma as to whether or not physical objects such as computers can be viewed as cyber objects.

A reasonable solution seems to be to separate the cyber and physical aspects of some objects such as computers. This way we would view physical aspects of an object such as physical box, weight, power consumption, etc., apart from it cyber parameters. By cyber parameters, we mean their functionality in and interaction with other cyber objects participating in cyber processes. For instance, if a hardware device is performing a certain function on a stream of data passing through that device, we would define a program that performs that function as a cyber object that is performing this process in cyber space, without looking into what physical elements this device is made of, how hard its body is, or what is its power consumption. This approach can help make analysis of events in cyberspace manageable.

To put it slightly differently, if we scan a computer for all the data contained in its memory, and then algorithmically describe the functionality of its components, we would have a digital copy of the computer, a cyber clone or a cyber avatar, if you will. This cyber clone or avatar is a cyber object.

It needs to be understood that, just as in physical space, an object can contain other objects. For instance, a data file is an object; a folder, a directory, or an avatar of the computer containing the file is also an object.

We will have return to this subject later, particularly when discussing some aspects of cyber attacks performed by embedding malware in hardware, such as modifying computer integrated circuits.

6.3 The Human Role

What kind of objects are humans in this scheme? They obviously are a part of the physical space, but are they a part of cyberspace? One answer is that as physical bodies they, of course, are not. But how about one's mind? How about a mind that wanders around cyberspace? Can somebody's mind be viewed as a cyber object? The answer is probably not, at least not directly. Indeed, our minds exist independently of cyberspace. They existed well before we even thought of cyberspace. Furthermore, our thoughts also exist outside and independently of cyberspace. We can only bring them into cyberspace through some kind of interaction with computers, or put them on paper and deposit the letter in a mailbox. In the latter case, the mailbox becomes a cyber object in the postal subspace.

Yet we still feel that we somehow belong to cyberspace. This is probably through a phenomenon that has been relatively recently introduced, at least in the Western world, known as the avatar. An avatar represents a human, whether true (think of something like a cyber copy or cyber clone), or partial (we only display our positive traits in social networks) , or altogether false. These avatars are definitely participants in cyberspace and can interact with each other and with other objects.

We will look into this aspect later, but it is extremely important to realize that in cyberspace we can study only a cyber object, such as somebody's cyber avatar. We cannot study a human user behind the avatar. Furthermore, avatar representation is controlled by its "master," or cyber user. Consequently, we cannot know how accurately this avatar represents its master—or even if it misrepresents him altogether. This aspect has important implications for security.

Cyberspace Participants. The next issue is to define the cyber participants. While a cyber object is a part of cyberspace, a participant may not be. For instance, a human receives data over the Internet. His mind is not part of cyberspace, but it receives and analyses data and perhaps makes some use of it. So the human is a user and thus a participant of cyberspace, while being actually outside of it. He can communicate with other users, avatars, and objects in cyberspace. So we can conclude that:

- **Cyber objects are abstract entities, passive or active, that participate in cyberspace functionality, and interact with other objects.**

There are a wide variety of objects in cyberspace; they can be divided into two major groups:

- **Independent objects**
- **Service objects**

Keeping in mind the main focus of this book we will use the term "object" or "cyber object" when we mean an independent cyber object, such as a computer or an avatar. The main difference between objects and service objects is that service objects exist to be a part of cyberspace infrastructure. Examples of such objects are objects that represent Internet routers and switches in cyber space, i.e., their cyber avatars. They do not represent cyberspace users, but rather are subordinate to entities that maintain and manage the Internet. They can be viewed as algorithms or mathematical descriptions of the corresponding devices' functionality, so we can see what function a particular service object performs on data traveling in cyberspace from one independent object to another. The study of service objects is a separate subject that is of interest to communications entities.

There are some characteristics of cyber objects that need to be recognized:

- **A cyber object may contain other cyber objects within itself.**
- **A cyber object may contain a private cyber space within itself.**
- **Cyber identity (public) is an attribute of a position in cyber space, and not of a cyber object itself. Different cyber objects can take that cyber identity at different moments in time.**

These characteristics of cyber objects, combined with observations we made earlier regarding dimensions in cyber space, lead to the following conclusions:

- A cyber object in public cyberspace holds a certain cyber identity at a given point in time, but further disclosure of this object's description is not mandatory.
- A cyber object can be a cyber object in more than one subspace.
- A cyber object can "shield" an unlimited private subspace from other objects in a given subspace. For instance, a computer connected to the Internet can be a part of another, private and unlimited subspace.

These qualities of cyberspace have a fundamental impact on security in cyberspace, and we will explore this area in later chapters.

6.5 Communications Channels

An important subject is the specific elements of communications channels. A cyber object needs data to be transmitted and received, ideally instantly and intact, i.e., with no distortion. However, this is not achievable at our present level of technology. Thus, cyber objects have to cope with data passing through a communication channel with certain latency and a level of integrity. In the Internet, this delay can vary from to milliseconds to several seconds, and up to days in the snail mail system. Or it can be lost in the channel, and the delay could become infinity. There are methods to reduce the delay, and these methods are improving, but from a cyber perspective, latency exists as a fact of the cyber infrastructure. So as far as cyberspace is concerned, the delay is just another parameter of a communication channel, and that parameter has to be considered in the interaction between the independent cyber objects. In other words, if a number of cyber objects are acting in concert, they simply have to make sure that communications delays are accounted for in their processes. This aspect may be particularly important in remote control of fast processes, or when a fast response is required for a specific situation in an otherwise slow process. An example of such a situation are the Unmanned Aerial Systems (UAS), the remote control of drone aircraft.

- **Since cyberspace is an abstract space, for independent cyber objects the physical technological implementation of a communication channel is not important.**

6.6 Data Integrity

Data integrity (or the absence of distortion) is another important parameter of communication channels. Similar to latency, distortion can occur due to imperfect nature of communications devices that comprise the physical basis of the cyberspace infrastructure. From a cyberspace perspective this is just another parameter of its infrastructure, i.e., the probability of data distortion in a particular channel that independent cyber objects have to deal with. If a given probability of data distortion cannot be tolerated, cyber objects can react to such imperfection of the physical space by developing and implementing mathematical methods of ensuring data integrity.

It should be noted, however, that implementing methods bringing data integrity to an acceptable level can be computationally consuming and will always take time. This will increase de facto communication delays. So these two parameters of communications lines need to be analyzed together so an optimal solution can be achieved.

6.7 Cyber Processes

Cyber objects can initiate and run processes, such as data processing, analysis, or run various programs, useful and harmful. Cyber objects also interact in cyberspace; their interaction is the exchange of data and information between cyber objects. This is the only way that cyber objects can interact with each other. However, this interaction can have a significant impact on cyber objects and, beyond, on the avatar's masters, the cyberspace users. Accordingly, a very broad definition of the term "process" in cyber space seems logical:

- **Any data processing or interaction among cyber objects and participants that happens within cyberspace.**

On a fundamental level, there are two processes that take place in cyberspace:

- **Communications (transmission and reception of data)**
- **Processing of data and information (any manipulation for any reason)**

This categorization is fairly universal. If we again use the postal subspace as a litmus test, a letter is transported and processed, i.e., read. Likewise, in the Internet subspace, a data unit is transmitted, received, i.e., communicated, and processed.

6.8 Communications

Communications is a complex process involving multiple objects. In the case of the public Internet, it involves at least two independent objects and at least two dependent objects. Independent objects may have different requirements for the process that involve such parameters as: a guarantee of communications service availability, guaranteed maximum latency, speed as a volume of transported data per time unit, and a certain level of data integrity. Fulfilling these requirements is far from a trivial matter. It may involve using a certain class of carriers, the development of multiple Internet access points, and the use of multiple carriers. It can also involve internal design of the independent objects involved in a way that would redistribute processing power between remote and local categories. We will review these issues in later chapters. Thus:

- **Processing of data can take many forms, the most common being data analysis and data transformation.**

6.9 Data Analysis

Analysis is probably the most common and complex process in cyberspace. Actually, this is involves a multitude of processes. Most of it is done within the independent cyber objects, and most of it is done on behalf and for the benefit of cyber space users, who are supposedly the masters of the cyber object as their avatars. We will take a closer look at different aspects of this process in later chapters, but for now we only need to realize that a particular analytical process can be either individual, taking place with a cyber object, or a collaborative one and taking place in different cyber objects.

6.10 Data Transformation

The second common type of data processing is transformation. This is a very common occurrence and constantly needed in cyber space. On a high level, we can think of the transformation of data native to one subspace into a form acceptable to an object in a different subspace. On a lower level, there are all types of "translations" of data from one format into another between different applications in a computer. Such translations are also commonly used as "bridges" between private domains of cyberspace and the public Internet.

While analysis is not regulated in the public Internet, communications protocols are. Thus any data that are intended to be transferred over the public Internet have to be transformed from whatever formats are used in independent objects and private domains of the Internet.

Obviously, breaking down every process into these basic bricks is not an efficient way to analyze anything. Interestingly, at the dawn of computer era, before the emergence of cyberspace, a similar integration process occurred. All computer functions were programmed in basic computer language. Then programmers started integrating commonly used programming tasks into larger "building bricks," and such languages as ALGOL and FORTRAN were developed. These bricks grew larger and larger, and computers became capable of understanding much more integrated commands, including limited voice interaction. This process has accelerated with the Internet. Now interactions include not only live digital audio and video interaction, but also action computer games in near real-time.

These interactions, however, can be subject to laws and rules of cyberspace.

CHAPTER 7

PHYSICAL SPACE AND CYBERSPACE—THE FUNDAMENTAL DIFFERENCES

7.1 Comparison of their Qualities

We are so used to our physical space that we often assume that its qualities, laws, rules, and peculiarities are true everywhere. This is actually incorrect.

Gravity. Take gravity. Gravity determines so much in our lives that we usually take it for granted, without giving it much thought unless, of course, one plans to take a tourist ride to the space station. In cyberspace, there is no gravity. In fact, there is no such a thing as "force" in cyberspace. Newtonian laws are not applicable there. There is no friction in cyberspace, except that caused by inefficiencies of its current infrastructure.

- **There is no gravity in cyberspace.**
- **There is no "force" in cyberspace.**

Distance. The next point to consider is that if there is no gravity in cyberspace, travel must be easier there. Travel, or moving objects from one set of coordinates in our physical space, is difficult and expensive. In cyberspace, it is much easier and not only because of gravity, but also because of distance. The longer the distance between the two points in physical space, the more effort it takes to get an object from point A to point B. But in cyberspace there is no "distance." Indeed, the difference between two coordinates in a dimension in cyberspace is just a difference between two numbers. Two computers with just one digit difference in their IP addresses could be half a world apart, while two other computers with several digits different in their IP addresses could be inches apart located on the same desk. We will return to this characteristic later, when we discuss latency.

- **There is no distance in cyberspace.**

Real Estate. Another difference between physical space and cyberspace is the goal of an attack. We often think of attacks in military terms, where the goal is a destruction of an object or capture of territory. In fact, most wars in the history of the mankind were for real estate considerations one way or the other, often thinly camouflaged as something else. However, while real estate was a strategic goal, the most immediate tactical goals were the destructions of objects, such as humans.

In cyberspace, real estate has no significant value. Remember, cyberspace is as big as we want and make it. The only exception is probably the domain name space, where value is attributed to some names. Destruction of an object in cyberspace can sometimes be a goal, but usually the goals in a cyber attack are different. For example, often an attacker wants just a copy of a file. The only corresponding situations in physical space are intelligence operations of one kind or another.

- **In cyberspace, real estate has no significant value. Cyberspace is as big as we want and make it.**

Visibility. We do not know how to make an object invisible in physical space. Let's take a look at "visibility" and "invisibility." Light is what makes an object visible. In order for us to see an object, the object has to either emanate light or reflect light. The concept may be easily expandable to other parts of electromagnetic waves spectrum. For instance, "radar visibility" means that in order to be visible, the object has to either emanate or reflect enough EM energy within a particular spectrum to be detected by a radar sensor.

In cyberspace, there is no light, there are no electromagnetic waves. What might be an equivalent is a stream of data that is transmitted to and responded to (i.e., "reflected") by a cyber object. An interesting aspect here is that an object can be visible only to those other objects that receive a stream of data from it. For those objects that cannot receive that stream of data it is invisible.

Invisibility. A very important conclusion here is that in cyberspace we can make a cyber object visible to some other objects by affording them streams of data, and invisible to all other objects to which we do not afford the streams of data from the object. This is a fundamental advantage for defensive technologies. In physical space, we cannot protect an object by making it invisible (the closest to an exception we have achieved here is the stealth technology that can make an airplane "invisible" to radar). We will return to this subject in later chapters.

- **In cyberspace we can make any cyber object invisible to all—except those we authorize to "see" the object.**

Identity. Traditionally, in physical space our identity is largely based on our name, date of birth, family history, Social Security number, driver's license number, job description, etc., and our address. In cyberspace, family history has no meaning. Cyber identity is determined by a full set of coordinates in a particular subspace. For instance, as we discussed previously, a file in a computer is a cyber object. It is an object in the IP subspace. This file resides in a computer with an IP address and may be associated with a particular application. In this case, the cyber identity of this file would be a full set of its cyber coordinates in the IP subspace: the computer IP address, its MAC address, a Port number associated with the particular application, and the file name would constitute the full set of cyber coordinates, singularly identifying a cyber object (our file) in cyberspace. An important point here is that not all cyber coordinates are public. The only mandatory identity exposed in cyber space is the public cyber identity. This public cyber identity is needed to make sure that data addressed to that object can be delivered. As we discussed in previous chapters, every object, like a computer, can also be a part of a private cyber space. Private cyber coordinates of a private cyberspace are not necessary for enabling the public services of the cyberspace.

- **Public cyber identity is a full set of cyber coordinates, singularly identifying a cyber object in public cyber space.**

Originals and Copies. This brings up one of the most remarkable qualities of cyberspace. In physical space, there is a huge difference between an original and a copy of something. Consequently, we have developed some effective methods for distinguishing between the two. Even so, we are very disturbed by the possibility of identical duplication, whether of a signature on a check, a contract, or an artwork. In cyberspace, this is not true. In fact, one of the spooky things about cyberspace is that there is no difference between the original and a copy of a cyber object. This leads to the fact that if a copy is correct, security systems based on object ID verification are not capable of distinguishing between the two. It means that a stolen identity can be used with impunity in cyberspace. If this involves a stolen ID of a person, a correct verification can only be made is physical space, usually after much damage has already been done via cyberspace.

- **There is no difference between the original and a copy of a cyber object.**

The following table summarizes the differences pertinent to security between physical space on our planet and cyberspace.

	CYBERSPACE	PHYSICAL SPACE
SPACE TYPE	Abstract	Material
Homogenousness	No, with homogenous subspaces	Yes
Space Limit	No Limit	Limited
Number of Dimensions	No Limit	3
Gravity	No	Yes
Distance	No	Yes
Object Travel (change of location)	Easy, free	Difficult, expensive
Object Size, Volume	No	Yes
Object Visibility	Optional	Unavoidable
Multiple Identities	Yes	Generally illegal

This relatively informal review of cyberspace, and the comparison with physical space, clearly shows that these spaces are essentially very different. In fact, there are more differences than commonalities between physical space and cyberspace.

In the following chapters, we will evaluate the shortcomings of our current security efforts in cyberspace and introduce a conceptually new algorithmic solution for cyber security.

7.2 Interactions Between Physical Space and Cyberspace

The most common interaction between physical space and cyberspace at this time can be broken down into two major categories:

1. Human utilization of cyberspace resources for satisfying data and informational needs;
2. Cyber-Physical systems or, as they are sometimes called, Supervisory Control and Data Acquisition (SCADA) systems, i.e., the utilization of cyberspace for automated control of processes, such as electric power distribution, traffic lights control, etc.

The first category is most familiar to the general population of Internet users. The second category is gaining increasingly wide acceptance as we delegate more and more important tasks to computers for making decisions and implementing them.

Both categories have a generally common set of requirements for cyberspace service:

- Data availability
- Data integrity
- Data confidentiality
- Process availability
- Process integrity

Let us review these requirements.

7.3 Data Availability

Data availability is essential for cyberspace users, whether they are humans or computers controlling some process. In some cases, data availability becomes critical, particularly in SCADA systems. These systems often depend on receiving data, and the interruption of a connection can have catastrophic consequences. Generally, data availability depends on availability of four factors:

- Communications channels
- A cyber object where these data exist
- Data within the cyber object
- A search engine for identifying the cyber object with the data needed if the source is not known a priori

We will examine these factors again later, in the context of security.

7.4 Data Integrity

Data integrity may have different value for different users. For instance, incorrect data for a casual Internet search for the best place to have a manicure done would be viewed as tragic event by very few people. However, incorrect data on temperature and pressure in a tank in a chemical factory that results in a powerful explosion would be viewed as tragic by most people. Data integrity can be compromised by the following factors:

- **Data integrity during the process of communications between the object-source of data and the object-receiver of data**
- **Data integrity within the object-source of data, where it may be compromised**

7.5 Data Confidentiality

Data confidentiality may be not important is some instances. For instance, when someone is searching for data contained in public databases, it is logical to assume that confidentiality is not required. An exception could be a case when a searcher is concerned with the fact of his search of some particular data, but in this case the concern probably relates more to confidentiality of the process than the data being searched for. At the other end of the confidentiality spectrum is the case of highly confidential government, military, or commercial data, where a loss of confidentiality could have grave consequences, including the loss of life. Data confidentiality can be affected by the following factors:

- Communications channels
- The cyber object-source of data
- The cyber object-destination of data

Data confidentiality in all these sites can be compromised in many ways, sometimes by methods that can be spread between these places. We will look at this aspect in later chapters.

7.6 Process Availability and Process Integrity

Process availability and process integrity refer to processing data that commonly takes place one way or another, either at the source or at the destination. In other words, cyber objects process data. Even if the data are not compromised upon their arrival at the destination object, it is important to realize that the process that is supposed to be applied to the data may or may not be available. furthermore, the process itself can be compromised. The result of a compromised process could be the same as with compromised data. For our purposes here, it is important to distinguish between the unavailability of the process and the undetected compromise of the process. If the process is obviously compromised, the resulting product will not be available, or at least the error will be easily detectable. However, the process could be compromised in a subtle way, so that the results are simply incorrect, but the error is not easily detectable. This case can represent a great danger and cause significant difficulty in finding and correcting the source of a compromise. We will return to this subject in later chapters, including its relevance to the so called "cloud computing."

Generally, there are two patterns in the interaction between physical space and cyberspace:

- Physical space/cyberspace
- Physical space/cyberspace/physical space

It is important to recognize that one physical space system's avatar can interact in cyberspace in many places, sequentially or in parallel.

An interesting aspect of subspace/subspace interaction and space/space interaction is that an object has to have control over its avatar. A physical space object has to have control over its avatar in cyberspace; simple translation does not seem to suffice because of the different natures of the spaces.

PART III
Cyber Security

CHAPTER 8

CYBERSPACE SECURITY

8.1 Attackers and Targets

A security measure is generally an action taken in reaction to a threat and in anticipation of an attack. That is as true in cyberspace as in physical space. As we discussed in Chapter 1, security here is limited to the area of subversive or clandestine attacks. Just as we excluded military-style actions from the security sphere in physical space, we will make the same distinction in cyberspace, particularly regarding the Denial of Service (DoS) attacks that can be relatively easily sourced. However, such attacks as the Distributed Denial of Service (DDoS), while being openly hostile, may be very difficult to source, so we will include them in our discussions.

In order to classify threats in cyberspace, we need to take a look at the origin of threats in cyberspace. In any space there can be native threats and threats that originate outside the space. In physical space, most threats are native.

Cyberspace, on the contrary, does not have native threats. Indeed, cyberspace was designed with no offense in mind. The main objective of the Internet, for example, was to improve survivability and reliability of networks and to facilitate the free exchange of information. As we discussed in Chapter 4, cyberspace is an abstract space. The only logical native threat is a threat of distorted data, for example presenting zero as one or vice versa. Since there is no native ill will in cyberspace itself, there is no security threat there—unless it is intentionally introduced by a human from outside cyberspace. So, logically:

- **All cyber threats are originated outside of cyberspace.**

We are not aware of any other space interacting with cyberspace, so the next conclusion is that:

- **All cyber threats are originated in physical space.**

This conclusion permits us to narrow down our security efforts:

- **All the threats must come through interaction points between physical space and cyberspace.**

However:

- **Once a threat, one way or the other, is introduced from physical space into cyberspace, it becomes a cyber threat.**

The cyber object that contains the threat is a cyber avatar of the originator of the threat in physical space. For example, a computer virus can be viewed as an avatar of the virus author.

The real targets of the cyber threats are objects, processes, and participants in physical space. Indeed, a hacker's real target is not a file in some computer. The goal is usually to inflict some damage to an entity, its ability to perform some process, to undermine its owner's well-being, steal money, etc. This means that:

- **Cyberspace and its objects and processes are not real targets, but a conduit for attacks originating and ending in physical space**.

But how does an attack that originates in physical space go through cyberspace and end up in physical space again? Through the proxies, or avatars. An attacker instructs his cyber avatar to attack the target's avatar. When the target's avatar is damaged, the damage is inflicted on the target. For instance, an attacker hacks into a computer that controls gas distribution to customers and alters files that control such distribution. The damaged program cuts off gas distribution to a particular customer. The attack path is: • **Originator (physical space)** → **Originator's program in his computer (cyberspace)** → **Target program in control computer (cyberspace)** → **Target customer is denied gas (physical space).** This illustrates the point that an attack enters and exits cyberspace through the links between physical space objects or participants and their cyber avatars. This point is well understood by malware writers, who disconnect their link to the avatar (releasing a virus with no recourse) in order to avoid detection and retaliation.

It is important to understand that despite cyberspace being an abstract space,

- **Cyber attacks are not abstract—they are real and are aimed at real physical space interests**.

Which brings us to the question: why are cyber attacks so popular and why are they increasing in number and power?

The answer is quite simple. Physical space has some built-in effective defensive barriers. For example, in order to attack a target, a means of an attack (a cavalry unit, an airplane, or a missile) has to travel from its location to the target. It would be a major endeavor for Lichtenstein to attack Texas. Natural defensive barriers such as distance and varied geography can require multiple types of transportation, substantial costs, and time, making such an option impractical and politically unpopular in Lichtenstein.

Cyberspace, on the other hand, does not have such barriers. So an attack that is impractical in physical space may become a distinct possibility via cyberspace. This means that **cyberspace is a convenient conduit for conducting an attack by one physical space entity on another, allowing and attacker to bypass most all the natural and man-made barriers and defenses**. The resources required to conduct a cyber attack are immeasurably smaller than those required for a physical space attack. This means that **cyberspace is a great equalizer of the participants**. Conceptually, the attacking capability of an individual can be on par with that of a country.

An interesting point here is that in order to conduct an attack through cyberspace, the target has to have a cyber avatar. For instance, if an individual has his particulars such as name, address, Social Security number, bank account user IDs, and passwords, etc., in his computer file, this file becomes his cyber avatar and can be attacked through cyberspace. If, however, a person does not have such a computer file, it cannot be attacked through cyberspace (of course, if a bank has his particulars in its file it becomes the person's avatar, authorized or not by the person and controlled by the bank, and that can be attacked through cyberspace).

This has a logical implication: **the more important the operations a country conducts through cyberspace are, the more vulnerable it is to attacks through cyberspace.** Consider two military powers in a combat situation. One is highly sophisticated with a lot of electronic gear controlling the disposition of its forces and communicating its intelligence via a satellite. The other one is well equipped, but old-fashioned, with little electronic gear. Something happens, like an electromagnetic burst of energy that renders all electronics inoperable. Which power incurs the bigger setback? Of course, the sophisticated one. The point here is that technological advances have to go together with security measures to ensure that the advantage is not easily rendered useless or, worse, turned into the disadvantage.

This is exacerbated by the fact that defensive measures are more demanding than offensive measures. The attacker chooses the time, place, and venue of the attack, while the defender has to protect against all the possibilities available to the attacker.

Furthermore, the attacker's capabilities are often not fully known to the defender. In the current status quo, cyberspace greatly favors attackers, who need not otherwise be very powerful, because cyber-savvy attackers can possess significant advantages over a powerful defender. In other words, **with the current status quo in cyberspace, attacking capabilities of a small entity or an individual can exceed the defensive capabilities of a powerful country.** This is an unsettling conclusion. To cure this disparity, we have to develop unsettling conclusion. To cure this disparity, we have to develop effective defensive measures in cyberspace.

Security of cyber objects. What is a threat to a cyber object?

- **Any potential interference that makes changes to the cyber object not intended by the object's owner is the generic cyber security threat to an object.**

- Thus, if someone intentionally downloads a picture file into his computer, this would be a change to the computer cyber abstract that was intended by the owner. However, the possibility that the same file can contain malware that destroys all the data files in that computer is a threat.

Methods for dealing with such a threat are described in chapters that follow.

8.2 Security of Cyberspace Itself

So far we have been looking at threats to parts of cyberspace. However, a very large portion of cyberspace as we know it now is represented by the Internet. The Internet serves as the backbone of cyberspace. If the Internet ceased to function, cyberspace would become a set of disconnected relatively small parts, and even if all its parts were functioning properly, most of the utility of cyberspace would be lost.

A part of the threat to cyberspace itself is a threat to its communications channels.

This includes both communications channels among the cyber objects and communications between participants and their cyber avatars. (It should be noted that cutting off communications is a subset of data modification when a certain set of data is substituted with zero data.) At one time, the capability to conduct such cyber attacks was the privilege of very few parties in the world, mainly a few government agencies. Nowadays hacking routers is a popular pastime of even some not-too-sophisticated hackers. Now that a greater and greater percentage of information is transmitted through cyberspace, this represents a very significant threat to society.

CHAPTER 9

LEGACY METHODS OF COMPUTER SECURITY

Having reviewed the fundamentals of cyberspace and security in general, we may now conduct a review of the legacy computer security systems. Let us take a look at our current defensive arsenal.

Experience shows that the current state of security is cyberspace is not adequate. Private and government systems are penetrated all the time, sensitive information is routinely stolen, and processes are interfered with. Yet as a society, we are more and more reliant on cyberspace for our needs in physical space. Furthermore, we entrust extremely important tasks to interconnected computers, and this trend is not slowing down—it is accelerating. Given this trend, the current situation with cyber security is rapidly approaching an intolerable level.

As the backbone of cyberspace, the Internet should be the focal point of our interest. Sometimes we hear the criticism that the original designers of the Internet did not provide adequately for system security, but this criticism seems misplaced. As noted

97

earlier, the fact is that the scientific and technical task for designing the Internet was to build a communications system that would be able to survive as a whole and maintain general functionality with significant portions of the system taken out by a physical event like a nuclear strike. Further into the development, the informational goal was to provide free exchange of information among network users. In other words, the goal was to maximize access to information, not to restrict it. The invention of packet switching as a communications methodology enabled the developers to achieve their explicit goals, which were precisely the opposite of the security goal of restricting access to information.

A further reason for the current state of security is that cyberspace is still such new phenomenon that we are only just beginning to understand it, and we have a long way to go.

Let's take a look at the legacy technologies utilized to provide computer and communications security.

9.1 The Firewall

The most common computer security tool is the firewall. As its name implies, it purports to fortify a computer or a network against network attacks. That is precisely the fundamental problem with this technology. Fortification is a feature of physical space, as we have described earlier in Chapter 1. However, fortification does not work very well in cyberspace. When a mainstream technology does not work for a number of years, common sense tells us that there must be something wrong with it and that we must try to find different approaches. The firewall has never really worked for a quarter of a century, yet for some reason we still desperately cling to the hope that, magically, the next firewall will work. It takes time and effort, usually about six months and a half-million dollars, for experts with advanced degrees in computer science to build a decent firewall. However, the reality is that it takes a high school kid, a PC, and a fortnight to break it. Indeed, most firewalls are broken during testing before they are delivered to the first customer. This is not good economics.

Let's take a look at the mathematics behind the firewall and see why its performance is so poor.

All cryptography as we know it today is based on a fundamental axiom that for any expressions **A** and **B**, there is always a conversion **P** that, applied to **B** would make it look like **A**:

$$P: B \rightarrow A$$

Furthermore, there are an unlimited number of such conversions, regardless of what **A** and **B** are. Instinctively, this is pretty obvious. For a very simple example, let suppose that **A = 8** and **B = 2**. In this case **8** could be represented as 2+6, or 2+7-1, or 2+8-2, etc., making **P** equal +6 or +7-1, or +8-2, etc.

A firewall can be hardware, software, or firmware, but for cyberspace it does not matter. Let us take a look at the firewall in cyberspace. As we discussed regarding avatars, in cyberspace the only thing matters is its abstract, i.e., its functionality, in other words the algorithm that the firewall is built to perform. Every System Administrator knows how to configure a firewall. By doing that, he establishes the firewall's cyber functionality, or algorithm. This algorithm is designed to allow certain communications to pass through and certain communications to be blocked.

A typical misunderstanding is when someone states that a firewall has a "security policy." This is not exactly true. A firewall does not have a security policy; it has a technical policy, which is to allow only certain complying traffic through and disallow any other traffic. In other words, the firewall is configured in a way that allows only traffic compliant with an expression **A**, i.e., whatever is configured by the Security Administrator.

Now, suppose that an attacker designed a certain script to do some specific damage if it could enter a target computer. That script is represented by expression **B**. If a firewall is configured properly, **B** will not be allowed to enter the protected computer since the firewall will only allow **A**.

When the attacker realizes the situation, and he knows what he is doing, he will try to determine what the firewall will allow through. In other words, he will try to find out the **A**. There are many ways to do that, and it certainly is not a difficult task; for instance, it can be determined by just watching the traffic the firewall is allowing through.

Suppose our attacker has found out the **A**. Now the attacker has to find the conversion **P** that would convert his attacking script **B** to make it look like **A,** so it would be allowed through the firewall. It should not be difficult since he knows that there are an unlimited number of solutions for this problem that would allow to convert **B** to look like **A**.

After the conversion is applied to the attacking script **B**, looking like **A** it legitimately passes through the firewall and enters the target computer. Now the task is to convert the **B** camouflaged as **A** back into the original and malicious **B**. This is a little more sophisticated task than the previous one, but again, we know that there are an unlimited number of solutions.

This simple exercise is a clear illustration that:

- **For any malicious computer script (code) there are an unlimited number of solutions to penetrate any firewall**.

P: B $\rightarrow$ A $\rightarrow$ [firewall] $\rightarrow$ P^{-1}: A $\rightarrow$ B

This is an expression of a firewall penetration during a computer hacking, where

B = any malicious script (code)
A = any firewall configuration
P = conversion that exists in unlimited numbers
P^{-1} = reversed conversion that exists in unlimited numbers

One simple example of passing an unauthorized protocol through a firewall is "tunneling" or "wrapping" the unauthorized protocol in an authorized protocol.

The conclusion from this expression is that:

- **Any firewall can be penetrated by any malicious code in an unlimited number of ways.**

This is a clear proof that, even conceptually, the firewall as a cyber security measure is mathematically flawed. No matter how much we want a firewall to be effective, it simply cannot be. This conclusion confirms and explains our long and frustrating experience with firewalls.

While "firewall" is a good marketing brand, from a technical standpoint it probably should be called a "fig leaf" solution. We really have to stop wishful thinking and find real solutions.

9.2 Password-based Access Control Systems

The widespread use of password-based access control systems can be explained by their simplicity and the instinctive sense of security they give to casual computer users. Password-based systems represent a rudimental crypto system with a primitive algorithm and an extremely vulnerable key.

In any crypto system, the major components that establish degree of protection afforded by the system are:

- Strength of the algorithm
- Length of the key
- Degree of the key's randomness
- Security of the key management system

Let us take a look at these components of a typical password-based system.

The algorithm is extremely simple and is known to the attackers. The length of the key is usually small. Discovering the key would not require any significant computational power or time, even if the key was perfectly random. In fact, discovering a password with a computer is much easier and faster than penetrating the electronic lock that we discussed in Chapter 3.

Furthermore, the degree of the key's randomness typically is poor. Any meaningful word or a phrase is pretty much worthless from a crypto viewpoint, even if one follows the "sophisticated" security recommendations such as avoiding spouse's, children's, and pets' names and birthdays. As long as a password is comprised of dictionary-based words, it's extremely insecure. After all, from a computer's perspective, our dictionary is really very short.

Key (i.e., password) management is another wide-open door into the protected computer. This is often true even for some sophisticated crypto systems. Casual users tend to be confident about their crypto protection. However, if asked where they keep their key, chances are good the answer would be, "In my computer, of course." This is a fundamental breach of security. A computer itself can be "broken into" in many different ways, and the key can be easily found. Let us say that a computer is protected by a password and a firewall. Either of the two represents an easy way in. If the key to a corporate Virtual Private Network (VPN), or a password for the user's financial account, and other personal information is in the computer, it all can be easily compromised.

To further complicate the situation, servers for companies and government organizations contain passwords of many users. Once such a server is hacked, the attacker gains access not only to information, but also to user IDs and passwords of multiple users. This can enable the attacker to impersonate different users, avoiding detection and inflicting significant and lasting damage.

9.3 Intrusion Detection Systems (IDS)

Significant attention to Intrusion Detection Systems (IDS) in recent years has been a natural reaction to the poor performance of the intrusion prevention systems, such as a firewall and password-based access control systems. Conceptually, this is not an ideal situation: we know our systems have been penetrated, and we are trying to find the intruder who is already inside, doing what he wants. It is a cyber equivalent of a medical autopsy, when the patient is already dead and an examiner is trying to determine what exactly killed the patient. It may be helpful for other patients still alive and the medical profession as a whole, but not to this patient. Furthermore, it may be a losing battle with a fast-moving epidemic. In cyberspace, we can easily have a fast-moving epidemic. In fact, it can move much faster than any medical epidemic. A vaccine is a preferable solution by far.

A common organizational system is a Network Intrusion Detection System (NIDS). These systems have improved vastly in recent years. They determine statistical patterns in the network and look for prohibited and unusual behaviors within the network. This is a useful approach that can detect some types of less sophisticated cyber attacks being performed through the network, hopefully detecting and disrupting them before they reach their target computers. However, in addition to the above-mentioned common problems with all IDSs, this approach has some inherent problems that inhibit its effectiveness and can potentially present a problem at the worst possible time. This can happen, for example, if an attacker exploits their functionality by attacking the IDS itself and using it for an effective DoS attack.

One fundamental difficulty in designing an IDS is that a process with a cyber object such as a computer falls under the same category as the malicious script we looked at while discussing the firewall. In other words, an attacker, knowing the principles of the IDS, can apply the same general technique he would use to penetrate a firewall. He can separate an activity that might trigger a suspicion into several benign-looking activities, and then combine the result later. A sophisticated malware can collect and analyze the statistics of the network and adjust its actions to make sure that each one of them stays "under the radar" of the IDS. Alternatively, an attacker can simply penetrate the IDS itself and either modify its functionality or disable it altogether, if only for just enough time to accomplish its mission. Penetrating the IDS itself is perfectly feasible.

A complicating factor for the IDS mission is the trend that applications running on our computers are becoming increasingly sophisticated and use increasingly sophisticated protocols. The user of an IDS is faced with a dilemma of balancing probabilities of false-positive and false-negative detections, i.e., whether to restrict allowed processes and face a lot of false-positive alarms or relax the requirements and face a lot of undetected intrusions.

Another vulnerability of IDS is that is can become the subject of a Denial-of-Service (DoS) attack. In this situation, the attacker establishes a computational advantage over the IDS. It takes an IDS more computer power to detect an intrusion than for the attacker to generate such an intrusion. A malware can be designed specifically to flood the system with a lot of "junk" that triggers numerous IDS alarms. The IDS can "choke" or may be turned off by the user. At that point, the attacker can start his real mission.

Yet another potential problem with the IDS is it inertia, which could be particularly dangerous for military or other critical networks. In an emergency, all the usual patterns within the network are likely to be violated. That in itself can trigger a drastic reaction from the IDS, which could be exactly contrary to the organization's goals at a critical time. In other words, even without any cyber attack, an IDS can shut down a network in an emergency. Given that in an emergency events are moving very fast, this aspect can represent a real danger. This danger is severe enough for a single important network, but it can spell a real disaster if it happens at multiple networks at the same time. The time required for recovery could be prohibitively high for handling the emergency.

Given all the difficulties that designers of IDSs are facing, probably the most fundamental conceptual disadvantage of the IDS is that it is an inherently reactive system. This is a big disadvantage in the highly dynamic environment of cyberspace.

9.4 Virtual Private Networks (VPN)

A Virtual Private Network (VPN) as a security device provides two functions in cyberspace: crypto protection of a private channel of communications and crypto protection of the transmitted data. Essentially, these functions are access security and content data confidentiality.

A VPN, if properly implemented and configured, provides much stronger protection against hacking than any of the systems reviewed above. However, there are some operational limitations that make VPNs vulnerable. Indeed, we keep reading in the press that networks of some large and well-equipped organizations have been hacked. All of them, undoubtedly, had quality VPNs properly installed and configured. Let's look at some potential venues for attacking a VPN.

Point-to-point VPNs are usually adequate to protect against most attackers. The exception is a case when an attacker has vast computing power at his disposal. Some years ago, this category was limited to a handful of entities in the world that possessed supercomputers or clusters of very powerful computers that could be deployed for the task. With that level of computing power, an attacker can solve crypto problems of the majority of VPNs. The attacker would compute the key of the VPN, which would allow him to enter the system through the VPN until the key is changed. We will look into this aspect a little later.

Now that the problem of hacking individual computers is becoming a threatening global problem, many hackers have created botnets for whatever purpose they choose. A botnet is a cluster of computers that have been penetrated and subordinated by an unauthorized party, and tied together to perform tasks dictated by their new "master." A botnet, if large enough and appropriately programmed, possesses considerable computing power. It is widely known that this computing power can be successfully used to perform a DDoS attack, and only primitive programming is required to orchestrate such an attack. What is less understood is that the same botnet can be used for much more sophisticated tasks, such as solving crypto problems of VPNs. This vastly widens the circle of potential attackers against organizational networks protected by VPNs. Initially, the botnets "belonged" to certain individuals or entities. Later, the botnet business model evolved into "renting" botnets. The competition drove rent prices down to very affordable levels for everyone.

The next evolution of the business model is probably going to be a botnet rental with "programmed-to-suit" service. This way a botnet owner would offer a service of configuring the botnet for a customer's specific task. Indeed, a customer may not possess enough expertise to use a general botnet for a specific task. The botnet owner, on the other hand, usually possesses a decent level of technical expertise that enables him to program and optimize the botnet for a specific task. So, business-wise it makes sense, but security-wise it is frightening. This could easily create a category of cyber-mercenaries with vast attacking capabilities. It would undoubtedly widen the circle of potential attackers further. Until now, most potential cyber threats have been limited to the "Capability + Intent (Will) + Opportunity" limitation. Such an evolution would practically remove the "Capability" component from the equation, leaving only the "Will + Opportunity" requirements. Furthermore, attack targets typically have a frequent if not constant presence in cyberspace, presenting an easy opportunity. This removes the "Opportunity" from the equation as well, reducing the equation to just Intent (Will). This could become a really dangerous situation.

Another weakness of the VPN is that the key is stored in the protected computer. This means that if a computer is penetrated once, malware can be deposited in it immediately. It should be noted that this penetration does not have to happen through the VPN; it can be done with a malware introduced through the local input ports of a computer such as a CD, DVD, etc. This malware would find the VPN keys and report to the attacker if the keys are changed, perpetuating the penetration of the computer.

Exacerbating this problem is a common practice that incorporates a firewall that bypasses the VPN and provides a bypass way into a network architecture. Such a practice is probably a bow to "user convenience," but the fact is that this often makes the VPN practically useless.

In addition to the above, VPNs have an inherent key distribution problem. Changing the key in a VPN usually is a logistical challenge. This problem grows exponentially with the size of the protected network. Synchronizing a key change in a significant system is yet another challenge. It should be noted that the key should not be changed "in channel" in any crypto system. If such a mistake is made, the attacker can concentrate on cryptanalysis of one particular batch of intercepted traffic, even if it takes significant time; at the same time, the attacker would continue his intercept and would store the transpired traffic. When the problem is solved and the key recovered, the attacker can quickly decipher the recorded traffic, tracking the subsequent key changes and bring his operation to real-time status.

These difficulties with the VPN key distribution systems are again amplified by the fact that in a large organization many people have access to the VPN keys. This in itself is a security weakness. However, this weakness becomes a real problem in the case of disgruntled employees, who usually possess the VPN key long after their employment has ended.

All these aspects of VPN systems limit the practical usefulness of a VPN for providing cyber security at the level required by modern-day cyber threats.

9.5 Anti-malware Systems

Anti-malware systems protect computers against cyber threats such as viruses, worms, trojans, etc. Their initial function is usually filtering traffic that tries to enter the host computer or a network. The legacy systems are based on a very large database of known malware.

The process is well established and employs many thousands of people with different levels of expertise. When a particular malware penetrates a number of computers and is finally detected, usually after inflicting the intended damage to those computers, it is analyzed, and a "patch" for threatened computer systems is developed. The malware's "signature," i.e., the image how this malware "looks," is recorded for future reference. The "signature" and the "patch" are added to the database and widely distributed to various organizations and computer users for adoption by their anti-malware systems. The anti-malware systems that received the "signature" would not allow this malware to enter their host. The system acts as a periodically updated firewall, with all the inherent problems discussed above. The process is repeated for every piece of malware detected. The database, naturally, contains data on millions of pieces of malware and is growing to an alarming size. The database, in effect, configures the firewall contained in the system that protects an individual computer.

This approach has significant problems: by the time the malware is detected, it often has already inflicted damage to numerous hosts. This is called a "zero day attack." By definition, a malware that is not yet in the database is not being stopped. This is becoming particularly dangerous since the malware is acting and proliferating faster and faster. The time to detect and process the piece of malware and to issue the relevant "signature" and "patch" could be too long to prevent its penetration into a very large number of hosts worldwide.

Only the malware that is detected by someone gets processed and catalogued. A lot of malware is not detected at all. For instance, a dormant malware is extremely difficult to detect. A prime example of it is malware embedded in cyber physical systems (or SCADA systems, as they are sometimes called) to be activated by a signal at a later date.

The user's protection is dependent on the ability to communicate, preferably all the time, with the database. The unavailability of the database for an update potentially can become a devastating malfunction for a large number of users.

The database itself and/or the updating process could be attacked and turned around to attack the customers' computers.

The process of dealing with the detected malware is cumbersome and expensive. Eventually, the user is paying for the system's inefficiency and ineffectiveness.

The second layer of the more sophisticated legacy anti-malware system is a check on compliance with protocols and rules. This is a process that also essentially represents firewall functionality. This can only detect crude attacks where the attackers did not bother or did not know how to present their malware in a way that looks totally benign to the firewall.

Obviously, these measures are not sufficient to protect a computer adequately. So a third part was developed. Periodically, at least once a day, the system scans the host computer files in an attempt to detect malware that has penetrated the defenses. This is a low-probability exercise. Malware that is already embedded in a computer is extremely difficult to detect. Furthermore, well-designed malware can and quite often does morph itself into different-looking items with ease, so even if an embedded "signature" is known, it is likely to avoid detection by scanning. Experience shows that scanning is not a very productive activity. The only consistent result of scanning is that the user pays for it with money and computer time wasted. In terms of inconvenience to the user, however, it presents a significant nuisance, is a lengthy process, and usually blocks a computer's use at the worst time, courtesy of Murphy.

9.6 Summary

This review of the most common legacy computer security systems clearly shows that each and every one of them is not satisfactory for the protection of cyber assets against modern cyber threats. They are reminiscent of a lock that works well against an honest person but is not much use against a reasonably skilled burglar. The common argument that these systems protect against "most attacks" is absolutely unacceptable. It sounds like the military statement that "We will intercept most of the ICBMs coming to town"– while just one of them can spoil the whole day. The truth is that the damage from just one cyber attack can be almost as devastating.

High-technology development is accelerating at a pace where a decade is the equivalent of eternity. Normally, if a technology has not worked well for three or four years, it is considered unacceptable and scrapped. But in cyber security, here we are with firewall technology failing to work adequately for a quarter century—yet we still are trying to resuscitate it. Common sense tells us to move on to something else, preferably to something that works.

One aspect stands out among these non-performing technologies: **all these technologies and systems are founded on the concept of fortification.** As we saw in previous chapters, physical and cyber spaces are so different that methods effective in one space are not applicable to another. So we need to develop approaches and systems that protect against cyber attacks by cyberspace methods.

CHAPTER 10

VARIABLE CYBER COORDINATES (VCC)

In the previous chapter we saw that the legacy computer security systems do not work very well in cyberspace—neither theoretically nor practically. The main reason for this is that these systems were designed and built using methods developed for physical space and then transposed to cyberspace. What follows here is an attempt to establish a fundamental base for the design of a new generation of cyber security systems. This base takes into consideration the actual qualities of cyberspace and suggests a new method of communications that provides security in that space. In other words, this is the basis for building security systems native to cyberspace, instead of importing them from the vastly different environment they were built for.

10.1 Cyber Coordinates

As we saw from the previous chapters, cyberspace has qualities defined by the following postulates:

- **Cyberspace is an abstract space.**
- **Cyberspace has no natural limits.**
- **Cyberspace can have any number of subspaces; we can build as many subspaces as we want there.** Examples could be such subspaces as Internet, telephone system, radio communications system with the radio call signs as its coordinates, etc.
- **Cyber subspace is not limited in a number of its dimensions.** For instance, the Internet has dimensions: IP address, MAC address, Port number, file name, etc.
- **Every dimension has no limit; it is as big as we make it.** For instance, from its initial implementation, the size of the telephone space has been increased many times. If need be, we can increase it again and again.
- **Every cyberspace dimension has its coordinates.**
- **Every cyber object has its cyber coordinates. Furthermore, it has to have coordinates in every dimension of its subspace.**
- **One cyber object can belong to more than one subspace.** For instance, our cell phone belongs to the telephone subspace, but it can also belong to the IP subspace and be able to function in the IP there by browsing and receiving e-mails. In this case, the object must have its coordinates in every subspace it belongs to.
- **Objects belonging to different subspaces can interact.**
- **Cyberspace objects can interact with objects in physical space.**

10.2 Cyber Identity

In previous chapters, we looked at the characteristics of cyberspace and saw the differences between object identity in physical space and cyberspace.

One of the fundamentals of offensive operations of any kind is that, before an attacker launches the attack, he has to identify his target. This is true regarding military operations, intelligence operations, criminal activity, and even business competition. In other words, an attacker must identify his target with an adequate degree of accuracy. Many different criteria are used to identify targets.

If an attacker targets a specific cyber object, at the very least he needs its full set of cyber coordinates, i.e., its cyber ID. This is not always readily available. Target identification has to start with the discovery of at least one cyber coordinate. When the attacker discovers at least the target's cyber coordinate in one dimension, he reduces the level of ambiguity and can begin preparation for the attack by trying to discover other coordinates of the target. Obviously, the larger the space and the more dimensions it has, the more difficult is the task of the attacker. For instance, in the Internet, discovering the target's IP address is a significant achievement, making the rest of the attack possible.

A different situation exists if an attacker is not interested in a specific target but is looking for targets satisfying certain criteria. For instance, an attacker may be interested in attacking all computers using a specific operating system irrespective of their IP addresses. In this case, an attacker would try to identify as many objects as possible satisfying the criteria. This method is typical of worm and virus attacks.

10.3 Variable Cyber Coordinates (VCC) Method of Communications

As we discussed before, the Internet Protocol (IP) itself was not designed for a high level of security and has proved inadequate to protect against cyber attacks. However, changing this protocol, given its acceptance and the investments in equipment that have already been made, does not appear economically feasible. This leads to the need for a supplemental security protocol, implemented within the existing parameters of the IP, that is capable of addressing the security concerns of our critical systems. This protocol must be designed specifically for the environment of cyberspace, i.e., it has to be based on cyberspace methods and technology.

Such an attempt follows. Let us take some derivatives of the characteristics of cyberspace.

10.4 Cyber Invisibility

As discussed in Part II, we do not know how to make an object invisible in physical space, but we can achieve just that in cyberspace. If an object cannot be seen by an attacker, it makes it difficult to attack. So let us instruct our object to reply and communicate only with authorized other objects. If a request comes from an unauthorized host, our host just would not respond. This technique would provide some measure of security, certainly against less sophisticated attackers.

To achieve that, we have to develop a set of parameters that would indicate the sender is "authorized" to communicate with our host. This could be achieved in a variety of ways, but we have to remember that in this example we assume the attacker cannot observe the "authorization" parameters.

If, however, the attacker is reasonably sophisticated, he would still find a way to detect our protected host. For instance, he can establish a position in one of the routers used for communications by the protected host and then pinpoint its position by watching the authorized traffic. Furthermore, an attacker can "spoof" his source IP address, i.e., start communicating with our host pretending to be one of the authorized hosts. Our host so far does not have any other means of distinguishing between a friend and a foe and would be duped into communication with the attacker. So the cyber invisibility would be useful, but it would not solve all of our host's security concerns. We have to come up with something else.

Furthermore, as is the case with a password, with some knowledge of the "authorization" structure the attacker can simply try different parameters until he succeeds in guessing the right set.

10.5 Cyber Travel (Agile Maneuver)

Why do we go through all the trouble of building walls? The likely answer is because we cannot move a protected asset out of the harm's way. So, since we cannot move an asset out of harm's way, we fortify it. Great. But in cyberspace, as we discussed in Part II, there is neither gravity nor friction. Furthermore, "cyber distance" between two coordinates also does not exist. This means that how far it needs to travel does not really matter for a cyber object; an object can travel in cyberspace without any of the difficulties and expenses of physical space. Furthermore, the size of cyberspace is unlimited, so there is plenty of space for a cyber object to move and avoid attack. So, if we change cyber coordinates of a cyber object from time to time, it would be more difficult to attack than an object with stationary coordinates.

Clearly, a moving target is much more difficult to hit than a stationary one. A cyber defense based on mobility and maneuver can certainly be more effective and efficient than a defense based on fortification.

10.6 Network Protection

Currently, cyber attacks that require a target cyber identity now enjoy "free" initial target identification. A request is sent to an IP address, and the cyber object responds.

Let's start with the task of protecting a single computer in a network. Suppose we are concerned about the contents of that computer, and we want only authorized computers to have access to it. Instead of fortifying it, why don't we just hide it from all computers except those authorized?

Suppose, our class C network has an IP address xxx.xxx.25, and our computer has an IP address xxx.xxx.25.135. The first thing we do is randomize its IP address. If this computer has to communicate across the Internet, i.e., outside our network, we have some limitations.

We cannot change xxx.xxx.25, because if we do, a legitimate packet addressed to this computer would not be delivered to our network gateway. So for our class C network we have only one octet within the IP address in the header to work with. A logical question is: what happens if we do not have any vacant IP addresses available on our networks? There are ways to address this issue, and we will attend to that later. For now, let us suppose that we have enough vacant spaces on that network so we have the space .1 through .254 to work with (.0 is the network itself, and .255 is the broadcast).

So we create a random number within the space of our network between xxx.xxx.25.1 and xxx.xxx.25.254. Suppose our random number is 45, and the .45 IP address is available.

We assign that number to the protected host and send it to all the hosts authorized to communicate with our protected host, and give that list to the protected host itself. Furthermore, we instruct our host to respond only to requests coming from our list of authorized hosts. This way we attempt to do two things: make the host cyber invisible for all except the authorized hosts and hide it (move it to a point in cyberspace unknown to the attacker).

All the authorized hosts can communicate with this host without any problem. Now, suppose an attacker tries to communicate with our host. If he knows the nominal address 122.144.25.135 he will try that, but he will not get a reply back because his IP address is not where our host is. If, however, the attacker suspects that we have moved the protected host, or he did not know its IP address in the first place, he will try to scan our network. He will get replies from all active computers on the network, except the protected computer that was instructed not to respond to IP addresses not on its list.

There are two important points here.

The first is that the protected host becomes cyber invisible to the attacker because the host does not respond to an unauthorized IP address.

The second is that non-response is a response in its own way. Not responding is not a standard IP reply, so the attacker can conclude that something strange is at that particular IP address of .45. In other words, we cannot hide a black hole. If the attacker knows our security algorithm of moving the host to a different IP address, he will justifiably conclude that this is the new location of his original target at .135.

So while an attacker cannot even start his attack on the target host, at least he's got an idea that the target moved to the new IP address of .45. There are, of course, many more sophisticated types of attacks that can overcome this primitive example given here for illustration purposes only. For instance, if an attacker penetrated a router between communicating authorized hosts (a so-called "man-in-the-middle" attack), he would know both the location of the target and the required source-IP addresses for the "authorized" hosts. That would be enough for a successful attack. A further conclusion can be drawn that in the man-in-the-middle attack an attacker can detect most changing cyber coordinates of the target. For instance, valid IP addresses and port numbers would become readily available for this sophisticated attacker. The attacker will have some limitations due to latency, which we will discuss later, but still this is certainly an opportunity for the attacker.

To address more sophisticated cyber threats, this embryonic cyber security has to be amplified. From the previous example, we should conclude that in order to address sophisticated threats we have to include other cyber coordinates in our algorithm, particularly those that cannot be seen even from the man-in-the-middle position.

So far we have been discussing only one cyber coordinate, the IP address. The security of other cyber coordinates has to be addressed as well. In order to communicate with a host, it is necessary to know its desired port number. We can apply the same procedure to the host's ports by randomizing their numbers and communicating the currently valid port numbers to the authorized hosts. In this case, even if an attacker successfully deals with the change in IP address, he will also need to know the valid port, making his task more difficult.

Not all cyber attacks come from outside the network. In fact, the most dangerous attacks come from within the network. Among many such possibilities, one type of threat is becoming increasingly common. For various reasons, mainly economic, many office building are shifting from wired LANs to wireless networks. In the wireless LAN environment, internal LAN communications often propagate signals beyond the building's controlled security zone, affording an opportunity for an attacker to intercept and interfere with the network's traffic. In this case, the attacker takes a position inside the network, i.e., behind the network-ISP firewall, where often there are practically no other meaningful defenses.

To address a cyber threat originating within the network, it is a good idea to protect the system's MAC (Media Access Control) address cyber coordinate. The same technique can be applied: randomizing the MAC address of a protected host and communicating it only to authorized hosts.

The important characteristic of the MAC address is that it can be observed only from within the network, but it is invisible to the man-in-the-middle attacker on an Internet router outside the network. So adding the MAC address in our algorithm would make an attack from the outside extremely difficult. However, the internal threat still exists, and we have to address it.

Let us take a tally. So far we moved our protected host out of the harm's way and hid it. Let us take a look at our remaining vulnerabilities. Our host is not protected from an internal attack because an attacker can see all the cyber coordinates that we changed. An outside man-in-the-middle attacker can see the IP address and the port number, but not the MAC address. Have we overlooked something here? Yes. Remember, an inside-the-network attacker can see *all* our traffic. It means that he can see all cyber coordinates that we sent to the authorized parties. This is definitely a vulnerability we have to deal with. Fortunately, dealing with it is relatively easy. We just have to encrypt our "control" traffic, i.e., traffic that conveys valid cyber coordinates to authorized parties.

Furthermore, suppose the attacker decided to change the contents of our control traffic. To address this possibility, we have to authenticate our control traffic cryptographically. This means that the content of a packet would be cryptographically processed so that any modification of the packet would be noticed, and any modified packet would be rejected by the recipient.

So now we change the cyber coordinates of our protected host and encrypt and authenticate our instructions to the authorized parties. This way we have covered most of the angles of attack, except one. A very sophisticated attacker can attack our encryption and authentication cryptographically. He can cryptanalyze our control traffic, and if he solves the problem, he can recover our encryption and authentication keys. This would reveal our control traffic, and our algorithm would fail to prevent this attacker from getting access to our protected host. Fortunately, we have a very valuable reserve here.

So far we have addressed the cyber security problem by hiding a protected host in a secret location within the multidimensional cyberspace and letting that location be known only to authorized parties. This is certainly better than a doomed "fortification" of the host. However, we still have a concern that the secret location can be discovered, either accidentally or by some sophisticated method of attack. Can we improve the host's security further?

The answer is yes. Remember, movement in cyberspace is relatively easy. Why don't we move this protected host from one secret location to another? This way we not only make the host cyber-invisible, but we make it likely that it stays cyber-invisible. If an attacker finds out the host's secret location, it would give him only a window of opportunity to launch an attack. This window will close with the next move of our protected host, making the attacker start pre-attack reconnaissance all over again. If we move our protected host often enough, we can create a situation where a successful cyber attack is computationally infeasible. In other words, we can make sure that the window of opportunity for the attacker is smaller than the time required to solve our crypto arrangements.

However, the attacker can counteract by concentrating on a sample of our traffic intercepted initially and just record all our traffic thereafter. After some effort, with high levels of computing power, the initial sample may be solved and all the following traffic could be quickly unraveled, leading to the real-time failure of our system. We really need to address this problem. The good news is that we can change our encryption and authentication keys in addition to the other cyber coordinates with every cycle. From an academic standpoint it is debatable whether the authentication and encryption keys are cyber coordinates or not. However, from a practical security viewpoint it makes sense to change the keys as well.

This would make any cryptographic solution by an attacker valid only for the time of the cycle. Furthermore, he would have only the time of the cycle to come up with the solution; later, the solution would be irrelevant.

In a man-in-the-middle attack, the attacker has penetrated an Internet router and has the ability to watch and manipulate the traffic through that router. However, a router typically has limited computing power and cannot be programmed to solve crypto problems. If the attacker wants to solve a crypto problem, he has to send the intercepted traffic to a computer base with a very large amount of computing power. The base hopefully solves his problem. But this takes time. After the solution is found, it has to be sent back for actual implementation of the attack. This operation can relatively easily be performed by a very sophisticated attacker on a virtual private network (VPN), since VPN keys are rarely changed. With our algorithm, we determined a required rate of "jumps," or the time of the cycle. Thus we can say that:

- **If we change the cyber coordinates of our protected host more often than the attacker's required solution time, plus the double latency, the attacker will have no chance of successfully attacking our protected host in cyberspace.**

With the algorithm we have described we can provide cyber security to a host by dynamics, i.e., by movement instead of by fortification. The standard IP cyberspace coordinates are assigned and generally fixed. For security purposes we can make them variable. So, to summarize, this is the VCC method of communications:

- **The Variable Cyber Coordinates (VCC) method of communications provides cyber security to objects in cyberspace by randomizing the objects' cyber coordinates and then communicating them encrypted, and only to authorized parties. The process is repeated frequently enough to**

make cryptanalytical solution within the cycle computationally infeasible.

In essence, this is a cyber implementation of the "need to know," the ultimate security principle. Of course, it must be noted that the *if properly implemented* caveat is fully applicable to this statement.

The description above does not specifically address the content data confidentiality aspect of security. In many situations, security concerns do not extend to the confidentiality of transmitted data. The current condition of a street traffic light hardly requires confidentiality, but the possibility of a hacking into the traffic control computer definitely does represent a threat. For these systems, it may not be necessary to address confidentiality. Thus the content data communicated between cyber objects (like computers) may or may not be encrypted, depending on a particular participant's requirements. It should be noted that the protection against hacking is not affected by encryption or nonencryption of the customer data contents. If data need to be encrypted, then the encryption keys also should be periodically changed.

10.7 Entire Network Protection

The next question is what we should do to protect all the hosts on a network. The question raised earlier regarding the availability of slots in any cyber dimension becomes important here.. We are trying to "hide" a cyber object in cyber space. Since cyberspace is multidimensional, we have to hide the cyber object's every cyber coordinate, i.e., its cyber coordinates in every dimension. This means that every dimension has to have enough space to hide every protected object. In other words, we need a sufficient level of entropy in every dimension.

The good news here is that cyberspace is as big as we want it to be. So we can artificially increase any dimension to the level that our entropy requirements are satisfied.

CHAPTER 11

CRYPTO ROBUSTNESS OF LEGACY VS. VCC METHODS

The VCC method of communications provides a superior level of cyber security. It also contains crypto characteristics that need to be analyzed and compared to the same features used in the legacy crypto systems.

Let us take a look at a traditional crypto system. Suppose we have an open text A. A system employs a crypto algorithm B that converts our open text A into a cipher text C. A great deal of research has been done to develop encryption algorithms. Many of the modern encryption algorithms are robust. However, each one of them contains a secret key. Most encryption algorithms are well known to cryptographers and generally assumed to be known to the attacker. Indeed, algorithms are often published to ensure a thorough testing by independent parties. Even if they are not published, they are traditionally considered to be known to the opposition, and justifiably so. This means that the whole operation of encryption relies on the secret key. As long as the key cannot be guessed or recovered, the encryption remains safe.

Two parameters make the key difficult to guess or recover.

One parameter is the key size. The longer the key, the more difficult it is to guess it. Naturally, if we know that the key consists of just two digits, it's definitely one of a hundred numbers, and it is not that difficult to try all of them. If a key consists of a hundred numbers, it may take a while to find the right combination. Computers, of course, make this job much easier. However, we have to remember that to convert our open text into the crypto text we need to apply our encryption algorithm, using the key. The longer the key, the longer it will take to perform the computation of the algorithm. This becomes a serious consideration when we have to encrypt a large amount of data within a short period of time. A good example of this is the encrypting of a stream of live video for transmission over the Internet. The tradeoff here is that we want the key to be long enough to provide security, but short enough to be processed quickly.

An attempt to recover a key by so-called "brute force," i.e., by trying all the possible combinations, is usually the last resort for a crypto analyst. Guessing the key could be much more profitable. For example, most hackers know that people usually choose birthdays, names, and the like that are easy for them to remember as their passwords (a password is a key).

11.1 Crypto Key Quality

Let us take a look at another aspect of the key, its randomness, which plays a major role. The more random the key is, the more difficult it is to guess it. Without going into the specifics of crypto analysis, as we mentioned before, it should be noted that designers of crypto systems spent many years trying to find a truly "random" process. Time after time, however, mainly due to our increasing computing power, the "random" process was found to have a period of repetition that makes it not really random but rather pseudo-random. In other words, the probability of the output of the random number generator (RNG) being a "0" or a "1" at any particular time should be exactly .5, as depicted by line **A** in Fig. 11.1. However, in reality that probability may fluctuate somewhat and look something like line **B**, pretty much repeating itself after a period **T**.

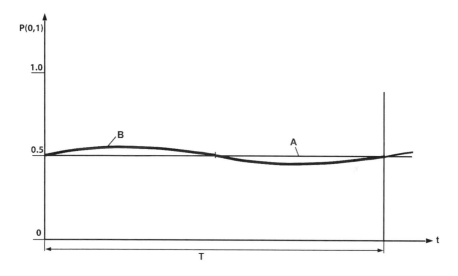

Fig. 11.1

With that in mind, random numbers generators that generate crypto keys in modern crypto systems are often rated in terms of time. This rating refers to the period of the "random" numbers' repetition when the random sequence is constantly generated. It actually means that if an attacker receives and analyses our "random" sequence, he will notice that after that time, the "random" sequence repeats itself. From that point on, the attacker, with some reasonable effort, can predict our key. This would render our encryption worthless. There is a direct correlation between the time to recover a key and the time to recover an open text. Given this, there are different requirements for the robustness of crypto systems. For example, tactical operational military crypto systems are often required to be robust enough to keep the message secret for the time interval between the message transmission and the end of the related action. At the other end of the spectrum, diplomatic and strategic government messages may be required to be secret for at least fifty or even a hundred years.

Theoretical aspects of this can be found in some applications of the Kotelnikov theorem. Furthermore, sufficient sampling of the output of the Random Numbers Generator (RNG) that actually generates the keys that can allow successful prediction of the crypto key based on a particular pseudo-random process can be derived.

Considering the above, let us compare the legacy and the VCC-based cyber security systems in relation to the pseudo-randomness of the key.

The enciphered output of traditional crypto systems often presents an opportunity to observe the random sequence representing the key. Many attempts are made to deny this opportunity, but they often have limited effect. In other words, a serious attacker would be able to record and analyze the line **B** in our Fig. 11.1.

A properly implemented VCC-based security system would behave quite differently. Indeed, the RNG is usually constantly running the process that generates a sequence of random numbers for the variable cyber coordinates. However, the amount of this sequence required by the system is not constant. In fact, even the user cannot predict how many computers are going to be on at any particular time and how many of them would be communicating. This makes the size of the required random numbers set "consumed" from the RNG largely unpredictable. The "man-in-the-middle" attacker would not have the opportunity to know how many computers within the target network are operating.

Furthermore, the VCC-based cyber security system does not have to change its cyber coordinates on a fixed schedule. In fact, a well-designed system would "jump" to the new set of coordinates at random intervals, making the consumption of the random numbers from the generator even more unpredictable. Fig. 11.2 represents consumption of the random numbers by a traditional crypto system as a solid line **B**, while the VCC-based system's random numbers consumption is represented by a series of samples Sj.

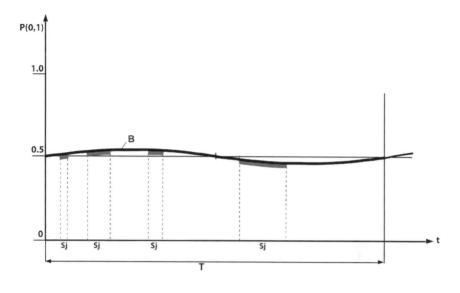

Fig. 11.2

This illustration clearly shows that it is much more difficult to restore the line **B**, which is the goal of the attacker, within the VCC-based cyber security system than in a traditional crypto system.

11.2 Crypto Key Vulnerability

Let us take a look at vulnerabilities of the key in a typical traditional crypto system.

A good way to present vulnerability is to view it as a product of the probability of a compromise and time of exposure. Indeed, if there is a probability of a key compromise, then the vulnerability increases with the time of exposure to that danger. For simplicity, let us approximate that increase as a linear function.

$V = P_c * T$
Where:
V = Vulnerability
P_c = Probability of compromise
T = Time of exposure

Without going too deeply into the details, let us examine the typical life cycle of a traditional crypto key. The first step is the key production. The key is generated and recorded ("manufactured") at a factory. This process includes some security risk. For instance, an attacker can place a RF receiver with a sensitive antenna nearby and record the generated keys through EM intercept. Or an attacker can have an agent within the facility who would somehow arrange production of copies of the keys for the attacker. Any event like this would compromise the key and ultimately compromise our crypto system. In all, this would represent key production vulnerability. Let us call the probability of the key compromise at this stage P_{kcp} (probability of key compromise at production). Also, let us take a look at the key vulnerability at this stage where the vulnerability is determined as a product of the P_{kcp} and time of production (exposure). It is represented on the following graph. The area under the graph represents the vulnerability V_p.

$$V_p = P_{kcp} * t_p$$
Where:
V_p = Production vulnerability
P_{kcp} = Probability of key compromise during key production
T_p = Time of exposure

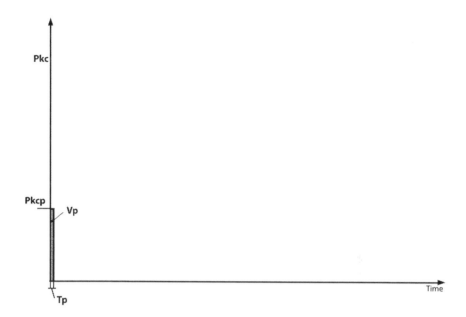

Fig. 11.3

The next step is the storage of the key in the factory's inventory. During this stage, the key is also vulnerable. For instance, it can be copied by a disgruntled employee or an attacker's agent. Let us call this key production storage vulnerability. Let us call the probability of the key **compromise at producer's storage** P_{kcps}. Similarly to the previous situation, **key vulnerability at producer's storage** is defined as the product of the P_{kcps} and the time of exposure. During this stage, the probability of a compromise is usually lower than during the process of production. Let us depict the result in a similar way and add it to the previous graph.

$$\mathbf{Vps = P_{kcps} * T_{ps}}$$
Where:
$\mathbf{V_{ps}}$ = Production storage vulnerability
$\mathbf{P_{kcps}}$ = Probability of compromise during storage at the factory
$\mathbf{T_{ps}}$ = Time of exposure (storage at the factory)

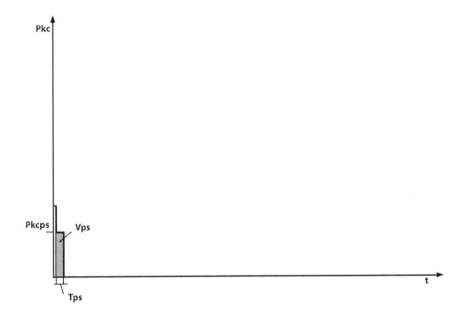

Fig. 11.4

The next step is shipment. During shipment, the probability of a compromise is usually considered higher than during the production stage. Let us call this **key shipment vulnerability V_t** and the corresponding probability of compromise during shipment P_{kct}. Similarly to the previous stages, let us add it to the previous graph.

$$V_t = P_{kct} * T_t$$
Where:
V_t = Key vulnerability during shipment
P_{kcp} = Probability of key compromise during shipment
T_t = Time of shipment

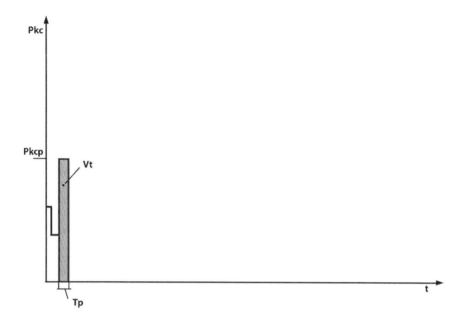

Fig. 11.5

The next step is the storage of the received key at the user's facility. Usually, the probability of a compromise here is higher than at the factory. Many users are not equipped and/or not trained to handle the keys in a secure manner. Let us call this **key user storage vulnerability V_s** and the probability of a key compromise at this stage **P_{kcs}**. Then:

$$V_s = P_{kcs} * T_s$$
Where:
V_s = Key vulnerability during storage at the user's facility
P_{kcs} = Probability of key compromise during storage at the user's facility
T_s = Time of storage at the user's facility
Let us add it to the previous graph:

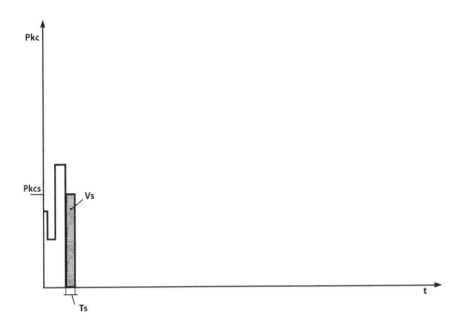

Fig. 11.6

The next step is to deploy the key and use it. During this stage, the vulnerability consists of two distinctly different parts: **crypto vulnerability** and **operational vulnerability**. Crypto vulnerability is determined by the fact that we now expose our cipher text to the attacker, and he presumably started his crypto analysis. This is an area where factors like robustness of the crypto algorithm, the key quality, and the key length are the determinant factors of the security, along with the capabilities, recourses, and will of the attacker.

Operational vulnerability is there because copies of the key now exist in different places. For instance, in many cases it is recorded in the protected computer. Furthermore, in many instances, like a VPN, the key is given to multiple users. Moreover, some of these users may be not as friendly as we think, or they may have already left the organization with the knowledge of the key. To amplify the problem, in VPN-like systems with multiple users, changing the key is expensive and difficult logistically. This leads to a situation that the key may be changed no more than once a year, if ever. This should be seen in the following graph where this vulnerability is added and the scale had to be changed to accommodate for the length of the key use. Let us call V_{kcuo} the operational vulnerability during key use and V_{kcuc} the crypto vulnerability during key use. Then P_{kcuc} is the probability of key crypto compromise, and P_{kcuo} is the probability of key operational compromise. T_{ku} is the time of the key use. Then:

$$V_{kcuo} = P_{kcuo} * T_{ku}$$
$$V_{kcuc} = P_{kcuc} * T_{ku}$$

Obviously, the combined **key use vulnerability** is:

$$V_{kcu} = (P_{kcuo} + P_{kcuc}) * T_{ku}$$

Where:

V_{kcuo} = Operational key vulnerability during use
V_{kcuc} = Crypto key vulnerability during use
P_{kcuo} = Probability of operational key compromise
P_{kcuc} = Probability of crypto key compromise
T_{ku} = Time of key use

The corresponding graph is represented below. Please note that the two graphs just described are depicted one above another, since the processes happen at the same time.

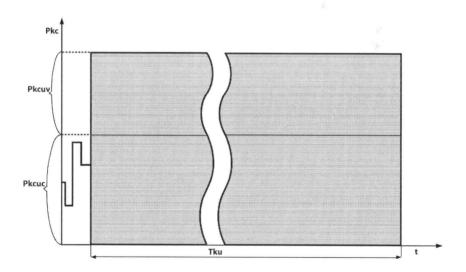

Fig. 11.7

A very important point here is that the time axis in this and the next graphs is not to scale. The reason is that the time typically used for the key is significantly longer than in any of the processes we looked at before. For instance, the reality is that few VPN users change their key once a year, and many of them never. So it is quite realistic to approximate the value of T_d as 1 year.

The final step in the use of a crypto key is the end of its use and its disposal. This is probably the most vulnerable time in the key's existence. Often, the keys no longer in use are not afforded adequate security. Sometimes the old keys are lying around for a long time or disposed of as if they had no value. In fact, they have great value. If an attacker had recorded previous communications, the old key would let him decipher all related previous communications. Let us call V_{kcd} the vulnerability of a key at disposal and P_{kcd} the probability of the key compromise during the key's disposal. T_{kd} is the time between the end of use and the key's destruction.

$$V_{kcd} = P_{kcd} * T_d$$
Where:
V_{kcd} = Key vulnerability during disposal
P_{kcd} = Probability of key compromise during disposal
T_d = Time between the end of use and destruction of the key

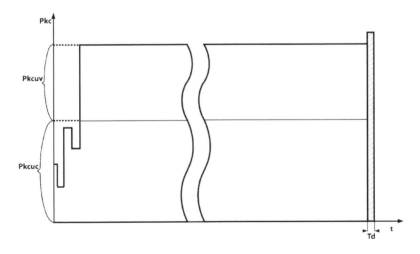

Fig. 11.8

134

The total area under the graph of Figure 11.9 below depicts combined key vulnerability of a typical conventional crypto security system.

Obviously, total key vulnerability vis-a-vis the discussed parameters is the sum of its components:

$$V_{kc} = V_p + V_{ps} + V_t + V_s + V_{kcu} + V_{kcd}$$

Let us compare it with the key vulnerability of a VCC-based cyber security system. The important point to consider is that a VCC-based system generates its own keys, and the first four stages of the conventional system are avoided altogether. Furthermore, the key is deployed typically within two jump cycles (changes of coordinates) after its generation, used only for one cycle, and electronically destroyed immediately thereafter. This brings a typical life cycle of the key in a VCC-based system to a time span of a few seconds or less. This compares very favorably with the life cycle of a conventional key of at least a year, giving it an advantage of more than 10^7. This is depicted in red on Fig. 11.9.

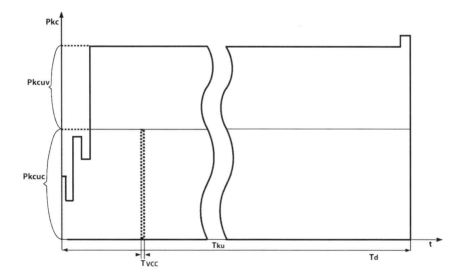

Fig. 11.9

So far we have examined two aspects of cyber security systems, comparing legacy systems to the VCC-based systems, and it becomes quite clear that VCC-based systems provide a much higher level of cyber security robustness. Let us examine one more aspect of security, which is not ventured into too often for a variety of reasons.

11.3 Impact of Latency

Latency is not important in attacking the VPNs because the attacker has plenty of time to execute the attack. However, latency has a significant impact on security of VCC-based cyber security systems. In fact, it increases security for these systems. Probably the man-in-the-middle attacks present the most significant and common threat to all security systems in cyberspace. VCC-based systems have an advantage in this case. Generally, they limit the time window of opportunity for the attack to the cycle time, i.e., the time when the cyber coordinates remain constant. However, the latency decreases this window of opportunity for the attacker because he must present the discovered piece of intercept (a crypto problem to solve) to a site with significant computing power. This takes latency time that in effect must be subtracted from the overall window of opportunity, reducing the time available to find the solution. Latency is also required for an attacking packet to reach the target (assuming the solution was found). Given that VCC-based systems can change their cyber coordinates easily every few seconds, man-in-the-middle attacks are ineffective against VCC-based systems.

By way of example, there was a report in 2008 that a group of enthusiasts using distributed computer power cracked a 3DES algorithm in about 4 minutes. This means that the key of a VCC-based system using 3DES algorithm cannot be solved if the system jumps even as slowly as once in 10 seconds.

11.4 Cryptanalysis Characteristics

For obvious reasons, cryptanalysis is not a very popular topic in the open literature. Without violating the tradition, let us examine the process conceptually, so we can understand the process without venturing into specifics. For many centuries, cryptanalysis was considered extremely important and was always performed by very few who were in the intellectual elite in their respective societies.

Nowadays, cryptanalysis consists of two distinctly different parts: a creative part that is performed by a small number of talented mathematicians, and a computing part that is done by concentrating enormous amounts of computing power working to find a solution to a problem experienced by some customers, using the algorithms developed by the creative group. In recent years, distributed computing has advanced to a significant degree, as has the opportunity to hijack a lot of computers around the world, tying them together in distributed systems of related computers known as botnets. This combination changed the cryptanalysis' paradigm: what used to be a privilege of a handful of governments in the world became a realistic possibility for appropriately inclined individuals and entities, becoming a great equalizer.

A simplified form the process can be viewed as follows:

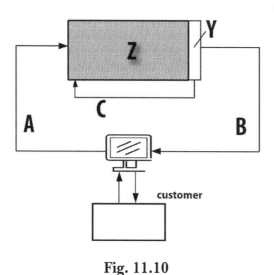

Fig. 11.10

In this representation, a customer somehow got hold of his opposition's encrypted communication. Provided that this communication is long enough to be worked on by a code-breaking entity, through an operator O it is entered into a black box **Z**. **Z** may be a computer, a cluster of computers, or a botnet. This computing power is programmed by talented people trying different variations of code-breaking techniques, and (almost) nobody knows what is inside of this black box. If, at some iteration, the black box solves the problem, the solution **B** is delivered to the customer through an operator O. If, however, the problem is not solved, it is returned automatically to the computing entity to try another approach (path **C**). Typically, the process is repeated many times until a solution is found and delivered to the customer.

The interesting point here is that, no matter what kind of operations are performed on the cipher text, the question is: how does the computer know that it has solved the problem? In other words, the computer needs to know its criteria of success. Otherwise, it would not be able to notify the customer even if the solution is found. This is why, no matter what is inside that black box **Z**, it must have a component **Y** that has to be able to detect that the problem has been solved (or substantially solved).

This determination is often made by statistical analysis of the result of the code-breaking attempt. We know that the cipher text is pretty much random, at least random to a high degree. So if the result of the attempted solution is determined by the computer to be substantially random, and it is rejected, the problem is shipped back to the black box to give it another try. If, however, the attempted solution is not random, the computer would know that it is the so-called "open text" the customer was looking for, and it is directed to the customer as the **B** (for Bingo!). The computer would know much more, of course. It would analyze the frequency distribution of the characters in the message and would probably determine what language the message is written in. There are numerous variations on this theme, but the main point is the same: the open text is not random, for if it is, the computer would not be able to distinguish it from an unsuccessful attempt and would keep working in circles indefinitely with no hope of detecting the solution.

This is generally how the legacy systems get cracked. **The most important point here is that the "open text" of a VCC-based cyber security system control traffic represents a string of its randomized cyber coordinates. It means that it is random or close to it. In turn, it means that the solution, even if found, cannot be detected by conventional criteria of success. Thus, conventional cryptanalytical methods are not applicable to solving VCC-based control traffic.**

11.5 Summary

In this chapter we have examined the crypto robustness of conventional legacy systems and compared it with robustness of VCC-based systems. Both key quality and key vulnerability aspects clearly favor VCC-based systems. But the biggest difference is, of course, in the cryptanalytical aspects of these systems. This simply means that current cryptanalytical methods are not applicable to VCC-based systems. Thus, **if VCC-based systems are properly implemented**, penetrating them over network connections is computationally infeasible.

This difference in robustness between the legacy and the VCC-based systems is fundamental. It is an inevitable result of the fact that the legacy systems were designed and built based on the methods of physical space. These methods are alien in cyberspace and are not effective there.

By contrast, VCC is a cyberspace method of communications, and it is native to cyberspace. Systems based on this method are naturally more effective in providing security protection to cyber objects and cyber communications. In fact, they are shifting the security paradigm in favor of the defender.

CHAPTER 12

VIRTUALIZATION AND CLONING

Virtualization is one of the most commonly used and, perhaps, overused words these days. By its nature, virtualization is a phenomenon of cyberspace. Closer to the purpose of this book, it has direct relevance to cyber security. So we shall here review some particulars of virtualization and its application in cyber security.

Virtualization is the act of modeling an object or process, physical or cyber, in cyberspace. For centuries, scientists and engineers tried to develop methods and mechanisms that would deal with very powerful and/or rare phenomena. For instance, to design and build a house that would have a better chance of surviving a powerful earthquake, one needs to experiment with various ideas of its construction. Constructing a building incorporating the next bright idea of an architect and waiting until an earthquake hit this particular building was not practical because the wait may be too long or the cost too high. So architects and engineers build a model of the concept house and vibrate its foundation with vibrations similar to those experienced in an earthquake, but on a smaller scale than an actual earthquake. They test the model against another model without the concept and determine if the concept house works better or not.

A similar situation is typical for naval architects. Building an actual new ship with potentially beneficial improvements is too expensive. Instead, they build a scale model of the proposed ship and test it in a small tank, essentially testing a scale model of the object and testing it in a scale model of the environment.

It should be noted that the scale model does not have to be smaller than the actual object. In a case of microdevices, that may be very difficult and expensive to build, so the model could be proportionally larger.

These examples are taken from the dawn of modeling just to illustrate the concept. What is really essential here is the fact that the model is an *approximation* of the actual object, i.e., not only it is smaller or larger, but it also represents only some of the qualities of the object. The science and, perhaps, the art of modeling is to build the model at a reasonable price so that the model is identical or very close to the object in *pertinent* aspects to the object. Thus the model is not a copy of the object; it is different from the actual object.

For instance, one can build a software model of a computer. By that, we normally mean that the model performs some algorithmic functions of the computer and sometimes even all of them. But we are not usually interested in how the frame of the computer would melt in a significant fire, so we do not include this aspect in the model. However, the closer the model is to the actual object, the more sophistication and cost is required to build it.

The development of computers opened a new era in modeling. Computer models became increasingly popular due to their economies of cost and time. Furthermore, computers made it possible to model processes that were totally out of reach earlier. A classic example of this is the computer modeling of the weather patterns where the results are becoming more and more accurate.

With the increasing power of computers, more and more sophisticated models of complex objects and processes became available. For instance, we test nuclear devices via computer models and trust their accuracy enough by building physical devices based on the testing of computer models.

The development of cyberspace introduced another era in modeling, and we call modeling in cyberspace virtualization. In just a few years of progressive development, we can conditionally divide virtualization into two distinctly different types. One is the virtualization of physical space objects and processes, often found in computer games and training applications. The other one is the virtualization of cyber objects and cyber processes. Typical representatives of this are virtual machines. It should be noted that this aspect often includes virtualizing of physical objects that is usually limited to computers' hardware functions. While computer games and training applications are an interesting field in itself, we will focus here on the second part, the virtualization of computers, including their hardware and software functions.

12.1 Virtualization in Security

A common example of virtualization is a virtual machine. It is a cyber model of a computer in another computer, often based on a different operating system. In other words, algorithms of a virtualized computer are imbedded into a program on the host computer. One host can contain multiple virtual machines. This technique can be very beneficial for many reasons and may become a cost-efficient way to enable functions of multiple computers in a single host. Usually such virtual machines are managed through a so-called hypervisor, a program running on the host.

Sometimes virtualization is perceived as a security measure resistant to cyber attacks. It should be recognized that virtualization per se does not provide security. Indeed, if a computer can be successfully attacked, so can its virtual model, since by definition of the virtual machine they both function by executing the same algorithms. Penetration of the host through a virtual machine would involve other steps and depends on how robust is the security of the hypervisor, but usually this is not an insurmountable task.

At the same time, virtualization presents significant potential for cyber security.

Cyber security systems based on the VCC, described above, can be very robust in protecting cyber objects against hacking, i.e., unauthorized access via communications channels. However, this method does not directly address cyber attacks that may come via such venues as other computer input/output (I/O) devices such as CD, DVD, and USB drives. This is an area where virtualization can be very effective.

Virtualization allows the building of a cyber model that is extremely similar to the protected object. For example, we can build a virtual "clone" of a computer that would be managed by an appropriate hypervisor. Any input to the protected computer can be tested on this "clone" that is monitored by the hypervisor. Running the clone would create an environment that triggers malware if it is contained in the input being tested. If the malware is contained in the input, the effects of its functioning would be detected by the hypervisor. In this case, the input in question would be precluded from entering the protected computer, the clone would be destroyed along with the malware, and a new clone would be erected.

Importantly, this method is not based on the "signatures" of known malware such as computer worms and viruses. In other words, instead of the flawed legacy approach of watching "how the input looks," it would concentrate on monitoring "what the input would do to the protected computer" if allowed in. This approach effectively addresses so-called "zero day attacks," i.e., previously unknown attacks or attacks that have not been detected and registered yet. By the algorithm of the legacy security systems, these attacks are let through. "Zero day attacks" are probably the most feared type of malware attacks, particularly for cyber-physical systems and financial institutions. This is described in the previous chapters, in our review of the legacy anti-malware systems.

This application of virtualization for cyber security is another example of using cyberspace methods for providing cyber security versus using physical space methods, as it is done by the legacy computer security systems.

CHAPTER 13

CYBER-PHYSICAL SYSTEMS

This chapter discusses the most real aspects of cyberspace and its impact on the systems that are a part of our everyday lives, i.e., where the effects of a security failure would be immediately visible and unpleasant.

13.1 SCADA Systems

Cyber-physical systems are also known as Supervisory Control And Data Acquisition Systems (SCADA). Cyber-physical term is a very descriptive term. In light of what has been reviewed in previous chapters, it means precisely that: an area or interaction between cyberspace and physical space. SCADA is an overly technical and somewhat vague term, but generally it means that the system contains automated control. In other words, the system is capable of performing certain functions without human control or intervention. For instance, a cruise control system in a car is a cyber-physical system. Turned on, it controls the car's speed without human intervention. This class of systems is extremely broad: it ranges from a washing machine to nuclear plant controls. However, conventionally cyber-physical generally means systems controlling processes in industrial plants, transportation, and the like. Although both terms seem to be popular, we will use mostly the cyber-physical systems term since it is more descriptive and suitable for cyberspace discussions, while SCADA is more reflective of the legacy systems of the industrial revolution.

These systems occupy a very special place: they are located at a juncture of cyberspace and physical space, largely without immediate human supervision. This is precisely what we have discussed in previous chapters, i.e., a cyber attack where the impact is in physical space.

From a cyber security perspective, computers can be put into two broad categories: serving humans directly, and controlling physical processes. It should be noticed, though, that even computers that serve humans directly often have cyber-physical components. The security distinction here is that if a computer serving a human for some reason malfunctions, there is some chance that this malfunction will be noticed and remedied by the operator. This chance is usually significantly smaller with computers controlling processes. This was recognized at the dawn of the industrial revolution, and engineers built redundancy into controlling mechanisms, sometimes multiple redundancies. For instance, a hydraulic system in an airliner has multiple redundancies in case of failure of one or more components.

Computers significantly advanced process-controlling mechanisms and made cyber-physical systems much more capable and widespread. Nowadays, entire factories, warehouses, and other industrial facilities are largely computerized, employing few humans.

Let us review some common types of these systems.

13.2 Industrial Control Systems

Most industrial processes are now automated. An example of the simplest form of a process is something like the temperature control of an oven or some chamber. A certain temperature request imposed by a human or another computer is supposed to be maintained there at a certain time. A computer controls the heater for the oven. As part of the system, this computer receives the temperature measured by a censor in the oven. A computer compares the temperature received from the censor with the temperature that is required. If the measured temperature is lower than required, the computer turns the heater on to raise it. This is called a feedback loop, depicted in Fig. 13.1.

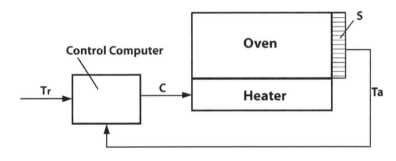

Fig. 13.1

In essence, the controlling computer performs a very simple algorithm:

$C = k(T_r - T_a)$
Where:
C = Control command required
S = Actual temperature sensor
T_a = Actual temperature in the oven
T_r = Required temperature in the oven
K = A coefficient pertinent to technical specifics of the system

When the actual temperature reaches the required level, the control command becomes 0 and the computer stops heating the oven. As long as the actual temperature is less than the required level, the control computer keeps the heat up, and the bigger the difference is, the more intense the heat that is applied to the oven.

Now, suppose that the sensor malfunctions and transmits a lower temperature to the computer than it actually is. The computer turns the heater on. The sensor still shows a low temperature. The computer keeps heating the oven, destroying the contents and, possibly, the oven. To prevent this, engineers often use redundancy: a second sensor that is independent of the first one and perhaps a second computer. A malfunction of both independent sensors or both computers is much less likely than of one. If the system is important or its malfunction may be dangerous, engineers add one or more layers of redundancy. As far as physical space is concerned, the problem is largely solved.

A cyber attack can induce this malfunction. For example, it can disrupt the feedback loop by disabling the connection between the computer and the sensor, or by disabling a sensor, or the computer. However, cyberspace presents a totally different level of security challenge in this situation. In a system with redundancy, a cyber attack can easily affect both computers, which can corrupt the process and can make it dangerous and destructive. This leads to a very important conclusion:

- **Cyber attacks can render redundancy ineffective**.

Furthermore, no matter how many levels of redundancy are implemented into a cyber-physical system, they can be neutralized by a cyber attack.

A common question: what can a cyber attack do to an industrial system? The answer is simple. A cyber attack can induce any malfunction that is physically possible in the system. Furthermore, a cyber attack can induce multiple malfunctions that are highly unlikely "naturally."

Modern industrial control systems are much more complicated than the example above. Computers control very complex processes, for instance in chemical factories, oil refineries, and such. However, the concept is still the same: they control a process based on the data and information available to them. Computers usually use multiple data inputs, which means they offer multiple targets for a cyber attack. First, all of these inputs could be impacted by a cyber attack either at the source or during communications. Second, the controlling computer itself can be compromised. Its programs running the process can be modified so that the computer sets in motion whatever control is wanted by the attacker, regardless of the data received. In the example with the oven, a hacker can modify the control algorithm in the computer, making it look like:

$$C = k(T_r + T_a) \text{ instead of intended } C = k(T_r - T_a)$$

From a program modification standpoint this is extremely simple: just change the "-" into "+." This minor modification can have major consequences. It would mean that the control command for heating would be increased with the increase of the actual temperature. The higher the temperature in the oven, the more heat the computer will apply to the oven, corrupting the process and probably destroying the oven.

Furthermore, a cyber attack can simultaneously disable the fire extinguishing system. In this case, the melted oven would not trigger a fire alarm and the fire suppressing system, so fire would spread freely to the entire building.

Another example of an attack on a relatively simple cyber-physical system would be a cyber attack on a modern car, if upon reaching a speed of 55 miles per hour the car's computer disabled the brakes and applied full throttle to the engine. This would make most drivers uncomfortable. (This vulnerability of modern cars to cyber attack is discussed in a University of Washington and University of California, San Diego study published at IEEE 2010 Symposium on Security and Privacy, available at http://www.auto-sec.org.)

Another interesting experiment was conducted at the Idaho National Laboratory, with the results discussed in the national media. An electric generator's control circuit was attacked via computer hacking, apparently disrupting the generator's speed feedback loop. The controlling computer was probably made to "think" that the speed of the generator was too low, when in fact it was normal or high. Consequently, the computer gave a command to increase speed and kept receiving the "low speed" feedback. It kept increasing the speed until the generator self-destructed. Once again, this was a simple target and a simple attack.

Another example of such an attack is the much-publicized Stuxnet computer worm. This computer worm was designed to impact the control mechanisms of centrifuges purportedly used for uranium enrichment by Iran. Having penetrated the controlling computers, it attacked the process. Most likely, it also attacked the centrifuges' speed feedback loop, leading to their damage.

As discussed before, in both cases cyber security systems were easily penetrated, and damage was done in physical space. This is the defining moment of attacking cyber-physical systems: an attack conducted through cyber space that inflicts significant damage in physical space. In both cases, however, the level of physical destruction was low. This is not going to be the case with many industrial processes.

In most industrial processes, relatively high levels of energy are present as part of the process. However, some types of enterprises contain very high levels of energy. For instance, in facilities like oil refineries, natural gas processing and distribution facilities, explosives manufacturing, chemical factories, and the like, a great deal of energy is present at any point in time. Over many years, engineers have learned much about the potential for accidents in such places and have designed industrial control systems that minimize the probability of an accident. Indeed, in modern energy-intensive facilities the probability of an accident is very low. However, occasionally accidents happen. An important achievement is this area is that even if such an accident happens, the level of damage usually is contained and is many times lower than the total destructive potential of the energy contained at the site during the accident.

This paradigm changed with the expansion of cyberspace. Many economic and operational reasons prompted the connection of industrial facilities to the Internet. For instance, the natural gas distribution industry wants operational data available to management, including top executives and the accounting departments, in real time. Practically, this can be done by connecting all facilities of a company to a single WAN (Wide Area Network) through a number of related networks. Economic considerations dictated connecting these networks to the Internet. It should be noted, though, that even if such a network is isolated and not connected to the Internet, it still is itself a part of cyberspace and is vulnerable to attacks launched from within the network. The point here is that cyber security vulnerability is not limited to Internet-connected facilities, and the idea of providing cyber security by having a separate network not connected to the Internet is largely an illusion. We will return to this important question later.

Let us review our physical space from an adversary's perspective, i.e., what is a target landscape that an adversary is looking at? Strategic military confrontation is a separate subject, so let us assume that the adversary is a terrorist organization based abroad. Terrorists are usually looking for targets that are highly visible because their priority is publicity. Secondly, they usually do not have means to deliver large amounts of energy, such as explosives, to the site. So energy-intensive enterprises make very attractive cyber targets for them. These enterprises already have enough energy on site to ensure total self-destruction, and any accident at such facilities invariably attracts a media frenzy, with high-profile political fallout immediately to follow. Furthermore, one does not even have to travel to the site to attack the target—this helps terrorists avoid the annoying inconvenience of dealing with the TSA. So energy-intensive industrial facilities represent an attractive target environment for terrorists.

13.3 Urban Services Systems

Urban services systems are rarely analyzed as a separate category. However, they represent a distinct category due to some features that are not often found elsewhere.

Any urban environment's most distinct feature is the concentration of humans within a relatively small area. Urban areas have always represented a challenge to engineers, demanding services in an environment with difficult parameters and restrictions. This actually concerns practically all services required by humans: power, water, sewage, traffic, medical facilities, food supplies, not to mention the critical importance of emergency services such as fire and ambulance. All these services depend on each other to function. This brings them together in a practically inseparable bundle.

The impact of a malfunction in any of the urban services usually exceeds many times the impact of the same malfunction in a nonurban environment. While these services are not as energy-intensive as many of the systems mentioned in 13.2, the impact of a malfunction is usually high. For instance, a simple malfunction such as a full power failure (with an emergency generator also disabled) in a skyscraper on a hot summer day can inflict significant damage. People can be trapped in elevators, offices will quickly become hot and uninhabitable, impacting people with health problems, and exit from high floors will be physically challenging while emergency crews will have a daunting task of climbing to higher floors and carrying emergency patients down through already crowded stairways.

It should be understood that an urban area is highly sensitive to a malfunction in any of its important services. This makes them attractive targets for terrorists. While physical aspects of security are addressed with a reasonable degree of success, urban areas are largely open to cyber attacks. An important aspect is that more than one target can be attacked simultaneously. For instance, a full power failure can be induced in several parts of Manhattan, and a traffic control system can be disabled at the same time, delaying or preventing emergency services' access to affected buildings. Such an attack could have a devastating effect in a city like New York.

This example shows that urban areas represent an attractive target environment for terrorist cyber attacks. Also, by permanently damaging urban services' controlling computers, a cyber attack can induce damage that would make recovery difficult, lengthy, and very expensive. A large-scale cyber attack can turn a place like Manhattan into a ghost town for a long time, with a significant loss of human life.

CHAPTER 14

CRITICAL CYBER-PHYSICAL SYSTEMS

14.1 The Power Grid

The North American electric power grid is highly integrated and controlled by computers. For many years, demand for electric power grew faster than our ability to produce it and deliver it to where it was needed. So we are constantly "underpowered" and trying to make the most out of the electric power that we have available. This puts ever-present strain on our electric power grid. The main reason for integrating smaller power systems into larger ones is the optimization of the distribution of electric power. It allows the channeling of power from areas of excess capacity to areas with a deficit. The idea is simple, but its implementation is far from trivial. Our electric power distribution system is very large and complicated, and it includes both US and Canadian power systems. A significant computer system controls it, and a lot of safety features are programmed into the distribution control mechanisms. Based on previous experience, the system is built with many automatic controls, but some radical decision-making is reserved for human operators manning the control centers around the clock. This works under normal conditions, i.e., when parts of the system may be under adverse weather conditions or subject to mechanical failures. The system has quite stringent redundancy requirements, so computer and human operators rely on the data received with a reasonably high probability that the data is valid.

However, even with its extensive safety features, the power grid system had a significant failure during the infamous New York blackout of 2003. It was generally attributed to a minor error leading to a domino effect, and the event showed that our power grid is less robust than we had thought. So the bottom line is that we have a large electric power distribution system with a highly computerized control system that is working at the limit of its capabilities, both energy-wise and computer control-wise.

This would seem to be an attractive target for terrorists. Studies have been conducted on the effects of losing electric power on a large scale. Interestingly, most studies concentrate on just the first phase of the effects of a power failure, and they have been shown to be extremely damaging in every respect: economically, politically, and emotionally, including significant loss of life. What is commonly missing in these studies is the subsequent phases of the impact, i.e., what happens if the power is not restored within hours or a few days at most. The reason for this omission is that the impact of a blackout's first phase is bad enough. But reality may be harsher. For instance, the usual assumption is that critical facilities like hospitals have back-up power generators. This is correct, but the fuel supply for the generators is usually limited, from twenty-four up to seventy-two hours. However, fuel resupply may not be available because it takes electric power to load fuel to the delivery trucks, and even if lucky, fuel supply trucks may be perpetually stuck in traffic jams due to traffic control failure. This is just one example from a long list of secondary impacts of a blackout. The conclusion is that a massive blackout could inflict severe damage to the country with significant loss of human life that could be further amplified by possible adverse weather conditions.

Let us now take a look at a possible cyber attack on the electric power grid. The power grid does not represent a difficult cyber target. It is controlled by computers, directly or indirectly with human input, and these computers are integrated in a WAN (Wide Area Network) connected over the Internet. These computers are protected by easily penetrable firewalls at best. Many of them are not protected at all because the devices are old, based on proprietary operating systems that are no longer supported by the manufacturer. Since firewalls are operating system–specific, it is difficult to develop one for such a device—even if the firewall worked. So from a cyber perspective, the electric power grid is a really soft target.

An attacker has many choices. For instance, he can simply disable the control computers or modify controlling algorithms in a manner similar to described in 13.2. This way, automatically controlled distribution starts malfunctioning in a major way. The attacker can also corrupt data available to human operators, and they would be bound to issue wrong or even destructive commands. Furthermore, an attacker can effectively destroy control computers so that their restoration or replacement and integration into the system would take months. Also, as discussed before, redundancy can be relatively easily neutralized by an attacker, removing the last hope of the defender.

14.2 Oil and Gas Production and Distribution

Oil and gas production and distribution systems represent a very important and significant portion of our critical infrastructure. Most people do not see it every day, but these systems are working very hard in the background. We take them for granted, but a slight malfunction in these systems immediately grabs our undivided attention. We need gasoline for our cars. This gasoline needs to be produced from oil in an oil refinery, stored somewhere for distribution, and delivered to the gas station. We need gas for our cooking and heating, whether it is natural gas or propane. That gas has to be produced, stored, and delivered.

One important aspect of this system is that storing energy is expensive. So, for economic reasons, only a relatively small (in comparison to consumption) amount of fuel is actually stored.

The storage mainly serves as a buffer between production, transportation, and consumption. This means that the system is really sophisticated and very sensitive to the availability and timing of deliveries and dispensation. In other words, an oil tanker arriving a few days late at its destination translates into significant economic losses. Similarly, a tanker having to wait several days to unload its cargo can reverberate through the system with profound effect. If many tankers are late, or cannot unload their cargo, this can have a major impact across the country.

Controls of processes at the industry's facilities are highly computerized, and those facilities are integrated into large systems connected through WANs communicating over the Internet. All these control computers are vulnerable to cyber attacks, as discussed above.

Several years ago, a house in a major American city blew up. Investigation revealed that it was a natural gas explosion caused by a malfunction when high-pressure natural gas was channeled to low-pressure pipes leading to the house. This odd accident illustrates how a similar malfunction can be induced through a deliberate cyber attack by a malicious hacker—or performed on a larger scale by a terrorist.

An attack can target process control computers, causing a malfunction that would not be mitigated by redundant safety systems, which can be attacked as well. This can result in a major fire, explosions, releases of volumes of toxic materials, and total destruction of a targeted facility. Even as a single isolated event, this is likely to result in significant loss of human life, with disruptions in fuel deliveries to consumers and a major economic impact. Extended to several facilities, the effect of such an attack can only be rivaled by a major military action.

The energy production and distribution industry functions like a complex and sensitive mechanism with very little tolerance for malfunctions. Numerous measures have been deployed to ensure the safety and security of the industry's facilities, and thus far these measures have proved to be reasonably successful. However, it does not seem to be widely recognized that a cyber attack can relatively easily bypass and disable those safety and security measures and can cause widespread major malfunctions with really disastrous results, not to mention the impact on the functioning of other industries and the economy of the whole country.

The conclusion of this chapter is all-too obvious: cyber-physical systems represent an attractive target environment for terrorists and other adversaries. These systems represent our major vulnerability to cyber attacks that has not been addressed by our legacy computer security systems. Taken together, these facts demand that cyber-physical systems should be given a very high priority for protection by a new generation of cyber security systems.

14.3 Financial Systems

As discussed earlier, the checks and balances method of bookkeeping, invented centuries ago, was simple and effective. A business owner employed different people for accounts payable and accounts receivable and made sure they did not collude. At the end of the day, the owner calculated the difference between the two accounts and compared the result with the cash on hand for the day. If there was a discrepancy, somebody had made a mistake or somebody had stolen money, and the owner knew exactly how much. This was a fundamental concept, and other more modern methods of bookkeeping are only variations on the same theme. The foundation of this is to separate some financial processes and to *independently* check the balance.

The main difference nowadays is that there is a large volume of rapid transactions. Computers can handle the speed and the volume. What computers cannot handle is the lack of *independence* in the processes. This is precisely what a hacker worth his salt can do. He can modify the data in the supposedly independent processes, so that the balance stays correct and the alarms are not triggered—while the money is diverted somewhere at the hacker's direction. Theft has occurred; detection has failed.

It appears that many financial managers do not understand this vulnerability. There are signs that criminals are ahead in understanding this situation. At least in one criminal case, the alleged perpetrators included a hacker and an accountant intimately familiar with a particular company's accounting system and procedures. The combined expertise of the attacking team defeated the *independence* of the processes and made it possible to avoid detection for a long time.

This is a fundamental defeat of the "checks and balances" concept that can be relatively easily achieved through cyber attacks. This is a much more effective financial attack than a conventional bank robbery, where a robber in the US on average yields a few hundred dollars and usually gets caught very quickly. Cyber attacks on entities with substantial funds can easily yield millions of dollars per attack, with a very low probability of detection, if the perpetrators know what they are doing.

The cyber security situation with banks is even worse. They are subject to the same technique, but more importantly, they are subject to systemic failures. Large amounts of money pass through banks every minute, and only a powerful computer can keep track of that. With all their efforts to avoid malfunctions, once in a while banks experience system failure, and it takes them at least a few hours to recover. Hacking the banking system is a little more difficult than some other systems, but it is quite feasible for competent attackers. A cyber attack on the banking system can destroy a system with all the redundancies as discussed above. Given the high level of integration of the banks into the national and world system, a cyber attack can potentially bring the entire country's banking system down, perhaps for a long time, because the banks' computers can also be effectively destroyed by an attack. The risk of contagion to other countries is very high.

It is important to realize that a successful attack on a banking system is not just something that can deprive us of the convenience of using ATMs for a few days. It can bring the whole country's economy to a screeching stop. In such an event, no transactions could be conducted, so there could be no shipment of goods, no groceries could be delivered or sold in supermarkets, and no gas could be purchased at the gas station. Patients would not be able to get their medications at a pharmacy, putting many at risk.

All this simply means that the financial system as a whole is a vital part of our critical infrastructure, and it is vulnerable to cyber attack.

14.4 Communications Systems

The Internet. Our communications systems are clearly part of our critical infrastructure. A greater and greater volume of our communications now goes via the Internet. However, it is not always understood that the Internet itself is vulnerable to cyber attacks. Several attempts at attacking the Internet have been made public in recent years. All of them were related to attempted attacks on several powerful computers that actually run the Internet. None of them succeeded, but one in particular came very close. Some experts interpreted it as a "dry run" by some unknown government to practice shutting down the Internet if necessary.

Ironically, all countries and, in fact, all attackers, depend on the Internet one way or another. This means that nobody in his right mind is interested in destroying it. What is more likely being contemplated is a typical government mentality: we want to be able to deny it to everybody, whenever we wish, except ourselves—we must have it available to us all the time. The questionable reality of this mentality aside, it means that an attacker would probably want to be able to shut down only a specific portion of the Internet. The practical implication of this is that we have to protect those computers running the Internet mostly from a limited number of maniacs.

The Internet infrastructure is comprised of networks, both backbone and local, and ISPs (Internet Service Providers). Without going too deep into this subject, let us just take a look at the routers that establish routing for the packets of data sent over the Internet. As a reminder, a router is a device that directs a packet of data down one or another route. Initially very simple, routers have become very sophisticated computers that make routing decisions based on increasingly complex algorithms. In a simplified form, a router can be presented like this:

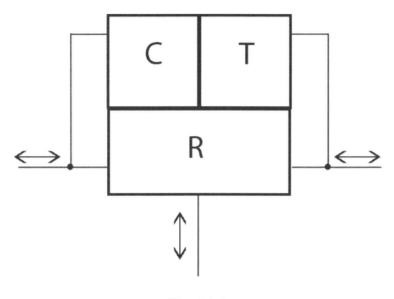

Fig. 14.1

Internet packets enter the routing part of the router **R** via a default port and are routed to another adjacent router. The top portion of Fig. 14.1 represents the service circuits of the router. The control circuit **C** is usually accessed through a separate port by the router's controlling body (owner), often a telecom company or an ISP. Through this circuit, the owner controls the router's functions, can change routing algorithms, and can upgrade the router's software. This is a crucial part of the router that enables whoever can get in to do pretty much whatever they want to the router. The third part **T** is the topography exchange circuit that enables a router to exchange information with other adjacent routers, so it can make more intelligent decisions on how to select a route for a packet with some consideration given to traffic conditions and the availability of the routes at any time.

Years ago, hacking routers was a privilege of just a few government bodies around the world. Nowadays any decent hacker can hack a router. This creates a real problem for security. By hacking a router, an attacker can perform many different disruptive actions, including:

160

- Intercepting all traffic through the router, establishing a man-in-the-middle attacking position. This makes attacking a specific target much easier for the attacker.
- Filtering any traffic, i.e., blocking passage of packets to or from any computer that communicates through that router, thus executing a Denial of Service (DoS) attack.
- Modifying any packets from any computer that communicates through that router.
- Flooding a target computer either with "junk" packets or multiple legitimate packets, actuating another form of DoS attack.

Attacking a router may enable a hacker to shut down, at least partially, a specific portion of the Internet. This means that protecting the control circuits of the Internet routers is a very important task for establishing cyber security. It should be noted that, indirectly the control circuits of the routers represent a typical cyber-physical system, which should be protected accordingly.

Telephone systems: Telephonic systems represent another part of our communications networks, but they are also run by computers, and many of those computers are connected to the Internet.

Some institutional customers lease so called "dedicated telephone lines," and they are under the impression this line is available regardless and is not subject to cyber attacks. What they do not realize is that the "dedicated line" is not a two-thousand-mile-long pair of copper wires. It is simply a regular line going though multiple electronic switches, and those switches are computers, many of which are connected to the Internet and thus are subject to cyber attacks.

In other words, our telephonic system is not immune to cyber attacks; it is very much subject to them.

These vulnerabilities of the communication systems should be understood in conjunction with the vulnerability of the other cyber-physical systems reviewed above. All in all, this means that we can not only lose a part of our critical infrastructure, we can at the same time also lose our communications, making recovery many times more difficult.

CHAPTER 15

CLOUD COMPUTING

Cloud computing is a fascinating concept that is intended to optimize use of computing power and intellectual property through the sharing of Internet resources. The concept was first introduced as "remote computing" in the middle of the last century, at the dawn of the computerizing of our society. In the 1960s, computing power was expensive and scarce. With few computers in the world, computing power and computer time was rationed very carefully. The main users were scientific organizations that wanted to take advantage of the new and powerful scientific and engineering tool. For most users then, access to a computer involved travel. With the introduction of computer communications, remote computer terminals proliferated.

That proliferation slowed down in the 1980s, mainly due to the introduction of PCs and rapidly declining prices of computing power and memory, and computer power expanding in accordance with Moore's Law. The development of new, sophisticated programming languages that were easier to use led to a large number of popular applications flooding the market, dramatically reducing the cost of such applications.

We now have a potential revival of remote computing, introduced under the marketing term of "cloud computing." Essentially, cloud computing is the delivery of computing as a service that combines computing power, memory storage, and programming performed at a remote geographic location. As conceived, this may be a different location for the same task at different times, thus optimizing the use of available computing resources at any given time.

This approach is attractive to some customers due to potential cost savings, though such savings are being eroded by the general trend of rapidly increasing computing power at declining prices. The cost of selling copies of already developed programming products is negligible. So current technological trends may reduce the potential market for cloud computing.

However, one major benefit of cloud computing is convenience. A user does not have to own a copy of an application; he can simply send the task to a provider, and somebody in the "cloud" performs the task and returns the results to the user. But it has to be realized that this convenience is subject to two aspects that need to be considered: reliability and security.

Reliability needs to be considered when a particular application must be always available to the user. If a delay is undesirable, the customer should make sure his network is reliably always available. If necessary, at least one back-up Internet access should be arranged, and that cost has to be considered. For instance, spreadsheet computations can be performed by the customer's computer during a communications failure if he owns the application. If he uses the "cloud" computing, he will have to wait until both the communications and the service are available.

Security is a requirement that is not as easy to satisfy as reliability. In turn, it can be divided into two parts:

One is **cyber security**. This means that if a customer considers the computing task itself and/or its results to be proprietary, it should only be communicated outside with adequate security at both the terminal providing the computing service and the communications process to and from that point.

The second aspect is **the privacy guaranteed by the "cloud" service**. For instance, a commercial company using a cloud computing service has to make sure the service requested is guaranteed to be performed at an acceptable point that is not connected to its competitors or cannot be publicly accessed. Otherwise, a commercial customer may end up having its competitor performing the task. Needless to say, this would result in an undesirable disclosure of proprietary information and make the results of the service highly unreliable. Individual users who want privacy have to make sure the service provider guarantees that processing and data storage are secure and cannot be accessed by unrelated parties, either via legitimate access or via cyber attacks.

These two aspects require clearing the "cloudy" status of the service and insisting on its transparency, with guarantees of both privacy and security.

PART IV
Coherent Defense Of Large Sovereign Cyber Systems

Chapter 16

PROTECTION OF LARGE SYSTEMS

Earlier in this book we reviewed the protection of individual cyber objects, and briefly looked at the protection of systems of cyber objects. We will now review the challenges to establishing an effective defense in the case of an increase in the size of a protected system.

16.1 Challenges of Increased Size

An increase in the size of a protected system usually leads to an increase in the number of entry points to the system, which present more potential penetration points for an attack. An Internet-based Wide Area Network (WAN) is a good example. In a WAN every one of its Local Area Networks (LANs) has at least one entry point to the Internet. These entry points may each have different levels of protection, but every one of them can be used to penetrate the entire system. Moreover, every LAN is also subject to internal attacks, i.e. attacks performed by outsiders from within the LAN. For example, an attacker can gain internal access to the LAN through the building's communications closet, typically located in the basement. Defense becomes even more challenging with the increasingly popular wireless LANs (WLANs). In WLANs communications signals very often can be received well outside of the physical security control zone of the enterprise. This drastically increases the number of points of potential penetration of the WLAN, and consequently to its WAN.

An increase in the size of a protected system also leads to logistical challenges in managing its security systems. For instance, the distribution of encryption and authentication keys becomes difficult, opening another venue for an attack.

Another problem is the fact that the larger the system, the more frequent are the additions to, and subtractions from, the network. Managing departing and newly added members of the protected system securely presents logistical and technical challenges, which grow along with the increased size of the protected system.

As we saw in previous chapters, our legacy computer security systems are very vulnerable even while protecting just individual computers. Their vulnerability grows approximately exponentially with an increase in the size of a protected system, making them easy prey even for relatively unsophisticated, routine attacks.

Security methods that are native to cyberspace, such as the VCC, offer the possibility of mounting dynamically changing multilayered defenses. However, even with this solution there are challenges. While the dynamic nature of such cyber security systems provides robust protection, an increase in the size of the protected cyber system increases the technical requirements for the internal exchange of information by the security system. The volume of such required exchange also grows with the increased size of the protected system. If the information exchange algorithms are not designed in a mathematically elegant manner, i.e. if they are mathematically clumsy, there may be an exponential increase in internal traffic within the security system. This can eventually limit or even choke the communications of the protected system, defeating the very purpose of the system.

Together these aspects present algorithmic challenges for the developer of cyber security systems, and a significant implementational challenge for the protection of large cyber systems. We can summarize the challenges of protecting large systems:

- **An increase in size of a cyber system offers increased opportunities for an attacker.**

- **An increase in the size of the cyber system leads to increased logistical and technical difficulties in adding and subtracting members of the system.**

- **An increase in the size of the cyber system leads to algorithmic difficulty for the internal communications of the security systems, which, if not properly designed, potentially can clog up the system's communication channels.**

These factors lead to the inescapable conclusion that an increase in the size of a protected cyber system presents more opportunities to the attacker, and at the same time presents inherently increasing difficulties for the developer of the cyber security system. This also amplifies the caveat of "properly implemented" as an essential requirement.

Chapter 17

SOVEREIGN SYSTEMS

The primary obligations of a sovereign state are the protection against threats to its citizens, its assets, and its territory, and the provision of certain services to those citizens. In a democratic country like the United States the government has an explicit and implicit obligation to protect its citizens, including their human rights and civil liberties. It is not an accident that all Government office holders in the United States are sworn to defend and protect the nation's Constitution, which includes the Bill of Rights.

17.1 The Protective Role of Government

The development of cyberspace, while presenting new and exciting opportunities, has presented numerous threats to US citizens as well as citizens of other countries. As we discussed earlier, these cyberspace threats are originated in physical space. These threats are now increasing in volume, severity, and sophistication. The natural response has been to increase the defensive and protective activities of the Government. Further protective measures by the

Government that specifically address threats coming through cyberspace are indeed urgently needed.

However, the increasing scale and power of the response to these threats also presents the inherent danger of the Government itself violating the civil rights of the people it is protecting. In other words, the misguided implementation of ineffective security measures (usually billed as absolutely unavoidable for security) often results in an encroachment on civil liberties of citizens – without any real security benefit.

Throughout the course of history authoritarian regimes, in their insatiable quest for power, have used every excuse to tighten their grip on their subjects. This trend has proved contagious for some bureaucratic elements even in democratic countries. It is important to ensure that cyberspace is not used for this purpose.

17.2 Cyber Security Does Not Require Encroaching On Privacy

The good news is that true cyber security, properly implemented, does not require encroaching on privacy. The very nature of cyberspace makes it possible to mount a very effective defense without violating any citizens' rights. There is no need for massive monitoring or sophisticated content analysis of private communications. Such invasive methods that jeopardize privacy are in the very short term only marginally effective and their cost is extremely high. In the long run massive monitoring or content analysis in communications channels are ineffective and often counterproductive in cyberspace.

An overzealous government can attempt to reduce the cost of its massive surveillance by forcing private cyber services providers into being government monitoring extensions, in fact doing the government's job of surveillance. In cyberspace this would be ineffective and even counterproductive. This kind of action would not only lead to increased political resentment toward the government, but the bullied cyber service can simply move its operating base elsewhere where its underlying physical infrastructure can reside in a less restrictive political environment.

In a democracy the owner of any information or process may restrict access to such information or process. However, monitoring of somebody else's private communications is invasive and represents a form of surveillance. It is no different from monitoring somebody's mail.

Oppressive authoritarian regimes around the world rely heavily on controlling their subjects' access to independent information in cyberspace. Governments are not always defenders of the public cybersystems of their citizens; they can themselves be attackers. Oppressive authoritarian regimes around the world notoriously rely heavily on controlling their subjects' access to independent information in cyberspace. As attackers, they will always have the advantage over the defenders.

17.3 Passive and Active Defense

Sovereignty is a flexible concept; it can change subject to time, will, and enforceability. Sovereignty is usually defined in a geopolitical context. Some commonly accepted characteristics of sovereignty are pertinent to security.

The principal characteristic of sovereign systems is their independence in decision-making; they can make the most critical existential decisions themselves, independent of other parties. Geopolitical considerations are restraining factors, but an independent state can still make such decisions. Nations can also be proactive in their defense. However, if we view this kind of sovereignty as absolute, there are entities at a lower level in a state's hierarchy that in certain narrower situations can make such sovereign decisions. Such delegated power enables them to defend themselves more efficiently. For instance, a state's military unit may have authority to defend itself by returning fire if engaged by an adversary. This would represent an active defense.

Another category of such conditional sovereignty might be a state's critical infrastructure, crucial for its existence. If attacked, the system can relatively easily obtain authorization and support of other systems, such as the state's military, to mount an active defense with available resources. So, the difference between a sovereign system and an ordinary system is that an ordinary system can defend itself only in a passive manner, while a sovereign system can either actively defend itself or easily obtain authority and power for such active defense. An example of such distinction is a difference between a merchant ship and a navy vessel on the high seas. While a merchant ship's only defense in a case of an attack is a faint hope to outrun the offender, the naval ship has the option to engage the attacker.

17.4 "Umbrella" Protection

The development of extremely powerful weapons, combined with the potentially sudden nature of an attack has led to a tendency for states to delegate more and more of their sovereignty to their critical systems, bypassing traditional decision-making processes. However, there is a growing body of non-sovereign, often private, systems which are part of the critical infrastructure of the country or perform otherwise important functions. Examples of such systems could be a natural gas distribution system or a power grid, or a private company that happens to be a defense contractor that may be very important to the country. These systems need to be protected as a matter of national priority; they need "umbrella" protection by the government. But that need creates a situation of high political and constitutional sensitivity if there is even an appearance of government interference with independent entities. This is not an easy issue to resolve, but fortunately there are certain characteristics of cyberspace that make possible the creation of an effective "umbrella" of security without involving such interference.

Chapter 18

SOVEREIGNTY IN CYBERSPACE

In our physical space sovereignty is a geopolitical concept. Every sovereign system is based on territory, political reality, and the ability to enforce and defend its sovereignty. So the question is, can we establish sovereignty and thus security rights and obligations in cyberspace?

Cyberspace does not have a concept of distance. Without distance there is no area, and further, there can be no national cyber territory, nor national cyber borders. So the conventional concept of sovereignty does not apply to cyberspace *per se*. Cyberspace contains independent cyber objects, but it also contains service objects that are definitely dependent. Indeed, cyberspace communications are based on the underlying infrastructure, which is in physical space, and thus is subject to the concept of sovereignty. This means that while there is no conventional sovereignty in cyberspace, its communications channels, along with the service objects, are still subject to sovereignty. Thus a repressive government can at least try to isolate or control some part of cyberspace by manipulating service objects under its sovereignty.

But we have to understand that these considerations are only conceptual. The reality can be quite different. Independent cyber objects are only cyber independent; they are simultaneously avatars of physical space objects or cyberspace users, which are themselves subjects of some sovereign power.

As we discussed in the previous chapter, it is the obligation of a state to protect its citizens and assets from threats. This protection should extend to the threats coming through cyberspace. To protect its subjects from cyber threats the sovereign entity must protect its citizens' avatars in cyberspace. Generally, this protection should cover not only the critical infrastructure, but should include protection of private subjects as well. So, we can therefore logically conclude that

- **A sovereign entity has a right and an obligation to protect its subjects in cyberspace, including providing cyber security of its subjects' avatars.**

This conclusion has far-reaching implications. For instance, it means that a state can use all means at its disposal for providing cybersecurity. The choice of such means to be used is at the discretion of the state. In other words, if some foreign entity, be it a state, a group, or just a hacker, mounts a cyber attack on, say, a private automotive company within the state's jurisdiction, the sovereign state, as a sovereign entity, has an option of mounting a devastating counterattack against the offender, ruining its cyber and physical capabilities.

An interesting situation develops when a citizen of country A is located in country B, and his cyber avatar is attacked by country B. Since cyberspace has no borders, it would seem that country A has the right, and perhaps an obligation, to protect its citizen's avatar in cyberspace no matter where this citizen is physically located.

Chapter 19

CYBER SECURITY OF SOVEREIGN SYSTEMS

19.1 Systems That Require Cyber Protection

Let us review the types of systems that may need cyber security protection from a sovereign state. From a cyberspace perspective there are four types of such systems:

Public systems – systems that anybody can access and utilize their services.

- **Commercial systems** – systems that are accessible and useable for a fee, available to anyone paying such fee.
- **Private systems** – systems that are accessible and useable only by owner's permission.
- **Government systems** – systems that are accessible and useable by the Government itself, or by its explicit permission.

In light of our discussion in the previous chapter, it is tempting to propose an "umbrella" protection by the sovereign entity to cover all these systems. That would be similar to the sovereign "umbrella" protection of a country against a military invasion. Let us review if and this protection is possible in cyberspace, and how it might be implemented.

- **Public systems.** Many casual cyberspace users have unrealistic expectations regarding their privacy. They release their private information into a public domain and expect it to be private. This is a fundamental misconception. By definition, if any information is placed in a public domain, it becomes public, i.e. anyone can access it. Furthermore, it can be copied and distributed indefinitely, so it cannot be revoked. In other words, an individual loses all control over any private information released to a public domain the moment such information is released.

It should be clearly understood that so-called social media are essentially public. They may create an impression that their systems are somehow quasi-private, but this is grossly misleading. As long as a system accepts anyone as a user without requiring valid cryptographical authentication and a positive verification of identity, it is public. Indeed, external cybersecurity of such systems is not even conceptually possible utilizing the legacy computer security systems. These public systems cannot use VCC-based security systems either, since by definition in order to be accessible to anybody willing to join, such a systems have to use fixed cyber coordinates. That makes such systems sitting ducks for any attacker. Internal cyber security in such public systems, such as virtualization and cloning, does not seem feasible, at least for the foreseeable future, due to the highly dynamic internal nature of such systems, and given the liberal acceptance of input policies that are essential to them. So to expect any privacy in social media is unrealistic.

Both users and the Government have to understand that these systems are a lawless cyber "jungle." Governments cannot protect public cyber systems; they can only use them, like everybody else, for "mining" information on a wide range of subjects as well as individual members. The only security service the Government can provide is to mandate a warning to potential users that whatever information they upload into such systems is likely to become public.

Government intervention in public systems may be warranted in a limited way. In physical space a democratic state can limit or prohibit those activities that harm its citizens. For example, local governments usually prohibit target practice with firearms in the streets of densely populated areas, and justifiably so. Similarly, in cyberspace a government can prohibit certain actions, for example, child pornography, but it should be recognized that enforcement of prohibitions is far easier in physical space then in cyberspace.

- **Commercial systems.** A system could be defined as commercial if it grants access to anyone who pays a fee. For example, many Internet-based databases and professional associations grant access to their resources for a fee to anyone. In terms of security, commercial systems may seem to lie between public and private domains. However, they are essentially public. These systems usually utilize some form of cryptographically weak authentication. But the decisive point is that they lack positive verification of identity. This means that anyone paying the fee will become an insider in the system, enjoying a cyber position favorable for launching an attack. As in social media systems, commercial systems exhibit highly dynamic internal activities, making it difficult to utilize internal defense through virtualization and cloning.

The reality is that privacy cannot be expected in public and commercial systems, including such services as email, browsing, and "cloud data storage". This is usually perceived as a political issue, but it's also a technical issue – it simply cannot be done, at least at this time.

- **Private systems.** Examples could be corporate networks, and public utility networks, such as those that control power distribution or control traffic lights in a city.

The fundamental cybersecurity difference between private and public commercial systems is that private systems can employ both valid identity verification and cryptographic authentication before allowing entry. This means that the system, to a reasonable degree, knows "who's who." This allows the system to employ VCC-based cybersecurity systems and thus provide a very strong defense against external and inside-the-network cyber attacks. Also, private systems usually exhibit less chaotic behavior than those that are publicly accessible, so insider attacks, i.e. those that originate with someone with a legitimate access to the system, can be addressed affectively by the virtualization and cloning described in Chapter 12.

However, while private systems have potential for effective cybersecurity, such systems are clearly limited to passive defense. This may or may not be sufficient when they are faced with extremely powerful DDoS attacks. Furthermore, their performance can be eroded by more modest attacks that are just powerful enough to slow the system down but not to shut it down. In other words, private systems are vulnerable to some forms of cyber attacks because they cannot mount a counterattack.

- **Government systems.** Government systems are similar to private systems, with the additional advantage of being sovereign. This means that they can have a strong passive defense, and usually have or can easily obtain permission and resources to respond with an effective counterattack.

As we saw in the discussion above, providing effective security in cyberspace to public and commercial systems is not feasible, at least at this time. Private systems are fully capable of having their own effective passive defense, but they lack authorization and ability to mount any active defense. Obviously, the protection of government systems, both passive and active, is the prerogative of the government. This leads to the logical conclusion that the optimal solution is for the Government to provide both passive and active protection to its own systems, and also to provide active "umbrella" assistance to private systems.

A very important question then is the nature and the extent of Government involvement in protecting private systems.

19.2 Data Processing Advantage

Cyber warfare, in its essence, comes down to a very simple proposition: the battle is about who has data processing advantage, which is a combination of superior algorithms and computing power applied to a particular engagement or cyber battle. In the highly dynamic environment of cyberspace the party at processing disadvantage will fall further and further behind, eventually losing the battle.

It should be noted that what matters is the processing advantage specifically at the point of the contest. For instance, with VCC-based cyber security systems deployed by the defender, the attacker has to go back to his base to do the computations, (which is usually the case with the man-in-the-middle attacks), so the effect of his processing power is reduced proportionally to the latency involved.

Another example of a processing contest is the misguided idea of defending against cyber attacks by monitoring defended networks and analyzing their traffic. Recognition of an attack in such systems is based on content analysis. Even if successful, which is a very big if, it takes significantly more processing power for the defender to detect an attack than for an offender to alter the particulars of the attack. Such disproportion would eventually shut down the defense system. This is also true for any attempt to analyze content at the service cyber objects, such as routers and switches.

Since monitoring of defending systems in cyberspace is not advantageous, the logical question is, what is better? Fortunately, cyberspace offers a solution: instead of the nonproductive monitoring of the defending system it is much better for a defender to monitor the attacker, i.e. employ active instead of passive monitoring. This can only be done by sovereign systems, and the next chapter will review how the concept of active monitoring of the attacker can be adapted.

Chapter 20

NATIONAL INFRASTRUCTURE PROTECTION SYSTEM (NIPS)

VCC-based cyber security systems offer an opportunity to establish a National Infrastructure Protection System (NIPS) that would provide strong protection to government cyber systems as well as "umbrella" assistance to the country's private systems. NIPS would perform near-real time comprehensive analysis of cyber attack attempts along with providing preventive, neutralizing, and retaliatory capabilities. Furthermore, NIPS would allow active monitoring of attackers around the world, which could potentially provide an insight into activities of potential adversaries in physical space as well as in cyberspace.

20.1 Active Monitoring of Attackers Is More Effective Than Passive Monitoring of Defenders

Simply put, active monitoring of attackers is more effective than passive monitoring of defenders. Very often the attacker is most vulnerable at the time of the attack. This can be clearly seen in boxing: a competitor is most vulnerable at the time he is delivering a blow. During that time he invariably exposes his own vulnerable points. Similarly, with the exception of some virus, worms and primitive DoS attacks, every time an attacker sends a packet to a target computer, he expects to receive a reply so he can continue developing his attack. If, however, an attack attempt is recognized early, especially during a reconnaissance scanning stage, a defender can deflect the attack from the target computer and send a reply that contains malware that can penetrate the attacker's system and subsequently report back to the defender, with the goal of securing intelligence on the attacker's operations. The malware can disable the attacker's computer or even his entire network if instructed to do so.

In more concrete terms, the NIPS would work as follows.

Both government and private systems could be protected by VCC-based security systems. The Government would control the security of its systems, while private systems would control their own security systems independently.

In VCC-based systems controllers register any attack attempts. For example, in Internet-based systems every packet coming from an unauthorized computer would not contain all the valid randomized cyber coordinates for the system and so would be immediately recognized by the system as an attack attempt and reported to the controller. An offending packet can be simply rejected, but it can also be processed for the purposes of active defense. First of all, it discloses the cyber location of the offender, at least the last launching point of the attack. Secondly, when there are multiple offending packets they can be statistically analyzed, and will define a pattern of attempted attacks. This reveals a list of attackers that might also utilize other venues for attacking the target, giving valuable intelligence for other aspects of security for the target. However, these two functions are about the limit of what an individual private cyber security system can do.

Now let us discuss what a collective cyber defense system can accomplish.

20.2 Analysis Centers

It may be advantageous to set up an analysis center. That can be set up on a geographic, industry, political, or any other basis convenient for the group of protected systems. Controllers of the participating cyber security systems would send their attempted cyber attack data to the center in near-real time. What is important here is that the data sent would not reveal any private information of the participating systems, but it would convey data on the attempted attacks and cyber coordinates of the attackers. This would alleviate privacy concerns of all the participants. The center would statistically analyze the data, revealing attack patterns on the protected group of systems. A large sovereign system would require multiple attack analysis centers set up for various groups of protected systems. These centers would report their data to a higher-level center for further analysis. Very large sovereign entities like the United States might require multiple layers of a hierarchy of analysis centers to handle the volume of attacks. This hierarchy would comprise a national infrastructure protection system (NIPS).

NIPS, as a sovereign entity, has the advantage of being able to employ active defense. Some analysis centers in the hierarchy can be equipped with counterattacking capability as well. If a decision is made that a particular source of attack attempts warrants further attention, the counterattack can be launched. Under VCC, the protected systems actually "own" their cyber coordinates and have a capability to assign them at will. This enables the system to "ship" the offended IP address if needed in near-real time. The system can "ship" the offended IP address to the counterattack unit of the NIPS and this unit can launch a counterattack on behalf of the attacker's intended target. If implemented properly, this technique can ensure a small risk of detection by the offender. This will enable NIPS to penetrate the "front" object of the offender's system immediately. Further penetration of the offender system, (once again, if implemented properly) can be achieved later and will allow deeper penetration of the offender's system.

It should be emphasized that the system discussed here can fundamentally shift the cyber security paradigm by assuring that a large sovereign cyber system has overall processing advantage over adversaries. Importantly, this can be accomplished within the realm of responsibilities of the sovereign power – and without encroaching on the civil rights of a country's citizens.

CONCLUSION

An obvious conclusion here is that we do not yet really understand cyberspace, and substantial work needs to be done so we can operate confidently in it.

Because we have accumulated a great deal of experience in operating in our world's physical space, we have become very comfortable in it, even to the extent that we are approaching the ability to destroy it. Given that experience, we have been trying to apply it to our operations in cyberspace, with the implied assumption that these spaces are similar. As our observations in this book make clear, this assumption does not seem to be valid.

Historically, many of the limitations and characteristics of physical space have protected us from major catastrophic accidents and attacks because they impose limitations on the attackers' capabilities, and we use these characteristics for defensive purposes. As our economy and our society grow increasingly dependent on cyberspace, we are only just beginning to understand how vulnerable that dependency makes us. Now it is becoming clear that cyberspace is fundamentally different from physical space. But as we have tried to clarify, the laws and rules of cyberspace demand a different mentality, and a whole new approach to personal, institutional, and national security. We have resorted to a diminishingly effective defense based on fear, force, and mutually assured destruction, when what we actually need is the implementation of new and different security technologies that effectively addresses the danger.

ABOUT THE AUTHOR

Victor Sheymov is a computer security expert, author, scientist, inventor, and holder of multiple patents for methods and systems in cyber security.

He worked for the National Security Agency (NSA) for a number of years and was a major contributor to the intelligence community of the Western nations. He is a recipient of several prestigious awards in intelligence and security.

Victor Sheymov is the author of *Tower of Secrets*, a memoir that describes his experience of the Soviet Communist political system and its repressive apparatus in the context of his career in scientific research involving guidance systems within the Russian "Star Wars" missile defense program, and then as one of the youngest majors in the Russian equivalent of the NSA, responsible for coordination of all security aspects of the Russian cipher communications with its outposts abroad. He and his wife and daughter were exfiltrated by the CIA in 1980.

Since finishing his work with the NSA, Victor Sheymov has been active in the computer security industry as the head of Invicta Networks, Inc., a northern Virginia–based developer of advanced cyber security technologies that address the protection of cyber systems, as well as programs to protect children and teens from Internet predators.

Victor Sheymov has testified before the United States Congress as an expert witness. He has been a keynote speaker at major government and private industry events like the NSA OPSEC Awards conference, a National Defense Industry convention, a National Science Foundation symposium, and has been a guest lecturer at a number of universities. He has also authored articles in the *Washington Post, Barron's, World Monitor, National Review* and other national publications. He has appeared in many national news programs including *Larry King Live, 48 Hours, Dateline, McNeil-Lehrer News Hour, Charlie Rose,* and the *McLaughlin Report.*

Victor Sheymov holds an Executive MBA from Emory University and a Master's degree from Moscow State Technical University, a Russian equivalent of MIT.

Made in the USA
Lexington, KY
17 May 2014